101 Recipes for Microwave Mug Cakes:

Single-Serving Snacks in Less Than 10 Minutes

101 Recipes for Microwave Mug Cakes:

Single-Serving Snacks in Less Than 10 Minutes

Stacey J. Miller

****

BPT Press
P. O. Box 834
Randolph, MA 02368-0834

LaVergne, TN USA
13 December 2009
166881LV00001B/56/P

Designed by Amy Ruth Seigal
and Peter Martin
Book cover by Kristine Kay Hanson
Edited by Ruth Loetterle

To Percy LeBron Spencer (inventor of the microwave oven)

ABOUT THE AUTHOR

Stacey J. Miller learned at a very young age that, on days when nothing else goes right, she could always make herself feel better by cooking an easy meal or baking a quick dessert. When she's not in the kitchen, she's indulging in her day job. A book promotion specialist, Stacey founded S. J. Miller Communications about 20 years ago. She is based in Randolph, Massachusetts and is a mom to the two best cats on the planet.

Visit the 101 Recipes for Microwave Mug Cakes:
www.microwavemugcakes.com

CONTENTS

ACKNOWLEDGEMENTS

I've been baking, cooking, and just generally making messes in the kitchen (and beyond, but that's a whole other story) since I was old enough to stand on a chair to stir the chocolate pudding. Thanks, mom, for sharing with me your love for playing, exploring, and learning in the kitchen, and for giving me the confidence to do it, whatever the results. How many mothers, besides you, would have eaten that mess that was supposed to be lentil soup when I was about 14 years old and had forgotten to stir it for two hours? None, and that's why you're you, and that's why you're the greatest. And, dad, for having a cast-iron stomach and trying so many of these creations, even before I'd half-figured it out, thanks (and apologies) are due to you, too.

Amy, your enthusiasm and support — and your great ideas and creativity — have been boundless, and this project wouldn't have gotten off the ground without you. I wouldn't have wanted it to. You're wrong about one thing, though. I love *you* more.

Scott: we have to work on your timing so that, next time, you can sample a freshly-baked microwave mug cake (in the flavor of your choice) made especially for you. I want a chance to redeem myself. And thanks for taking that one nibble, anyway. If there are any dental bills associated with your act of kindness, you know where to forward them.

Alyssa, every time I was tempted to just add a "glop" of something instead of measuring it, I harkened back to that time we made blintzes together — and I got to work, measuring things properly and scientifically. Thanks for the prodding.

Jessica, you were also an inspiration. I'll never reach your level of color-coded cool — but when the kitchen was a wreck, slowing down, taking a deep breath, and asking myself "What would Jessica do?" always seemed to help.

Barbara, thanks for being the first to send me that wonderful recipe for baking a chocolate mug cake in the microwave. And, Pat, thank you for posting a link to that chocolate mug cake recipe on your Facebook account at exactly the right time. You both helped line up the stars for me.

Finally, Steve, thank you for grabbing the proverbial ball and tossing it over the metaphorical fence with me for so many hours. You began to generate ideas (faster than I could commit them to writing, as usual) the moment I shared the microwave mug cakes concept with you. I could have done it on my own, but it wouldn't have been nearly as much fun. Also, I'm not sure how you ever convinced Ruth, Noah, and Audrey to turn themselves into front-line beta microwave mug cake testers, but I do greatly appreciate their contributions to the cause — and I hope Audrey's little mishap with her first microwave mug cake experiment didn't cost you a mug that your family truly cared about.

INTRODUCTION

The story starts one evening, about a year ago, when we needed a homemade brownie. We are not big brownie eaters. We didn't want a pan of brownies. We wanted just one.

As far as we knew, if one wanted a single homemade brownie, one had to bake an entire batch of brownies. So we did, and we spent much of the next day complaining about the futility of making a so-so batch of brownies, eating only one, and throwing the rest away.

Barbara, a friend (and fellow cat lover) who lives nearly 3,000 miles away, quietly emailed us a recipe she'd found online, by an anonymous source, for a single-serving chocolate mug cake that one could make in the microwave in less than five minutes. We tucked the recipe away for another time. Months later, an old college buddy, Pat, posted a link to the same recipe on his Facebook page.

We tried the chocolate mug cake. We liked it.

Sure, we quibbled with some of the details of the recipe. For example, the original recipe apparently promised to take less than five minutes to prepare. That was fine, if you didn't plan to spend time *really* stirring the ingredients so you'd wind up with no lumps. Also, our microwave didn't cook anything in the prescribed 2 - 3 minutes. But that was okay ... with a little bit of experimentation, we were able to create a chocolate mug cake, based on the recipe, that really worked well and satisfied that "I want a homemade brownie right *now*!" sensation.

Did that satisfy us? No, that did not. It only led us to scour the Net for more microwave mug cake recipes. We came up dry, and we were depressed.

How could the Internet do that to us? How could it provide us with a wonderful and miraculous recipe that whetted our appetite for similar recipes, and then leave us unhappier and more bereft (microwave mug cake-wise) than we'd been before? The Net had teased us, and it just didn't seem right.

We asked ourselves: Was this really all there was? Or were there more microwave mug cakes out there, just waiting for someone to invent them? Was it even possible to create new microwave mug cakes? What would it take to invent them? Did we have the necessary fortitude and pioneering spirit — and a microwave oven that was sturdy enough for the task?

The answers to those provocative questions led us to create *101 Recipes for Microwave Mug Cakes*. It also led us to nearly destroy several of our favorite mugs — and teeth — but that was before we perfected each of our microwave mug cakes (with the help of our intrepid MMC testers about whom we cannot speak highly enough, and upon whom we cannot lavish nearly enough praise or gratitude).

Within these pages, you'll find a wealth of delicacies that, we hope, nearly everyone (exempting true kitchenphobes) can easily and quickly prepare.

Microwave ovens are tricky beasts. We recommend that you stick closely to our recipes as well as our instructions for preparation. Please *read* those instructions. Our microwave oven suffered so that yours won't have to.

When's a good time to bake a microwave mug cake?

- When you want a snack
- When you deserve a reward
- When everyone wants a different flavor
- When you want something homemade
- When it's too hot to turn on the oven
- When it's too cold to go out and buy something
- When a whole cake is too much
- When you're trying to impress someone
- When you have a late night
- When you want to make somebody feel special
- When you need a lift
- On Monday morning
- When someone drops by unexpectedly and you need something to serve
- When you want to cheer someone up
- When you want to say "well done"
- When you want to say "thank you"
- When you want to say "I'm sorry"

It truly doesn't take any special skills or talents to bake a remarkably delicious microwave mug cake. It does, however, take a pantry that's stocked with the MMC-baking basics:

- all-purpose flour
- granulated sugar
- unsweetened cocoa powder
- instant puddings (unprepared)
- instant gelatins (unprepared)
- 1% milk (or soy milk)
- eggs
- baking powder

- vanilla extract
- prepared puddings
- yogurt
- cooking oil (we prefer canola)

You'll find specific MMC recipes that require other ingredients such as fruit juice, pie filling, peanut butter, jelly, baby food (sorry, but it's the truth), Crystal Light powder, and the like. The more ingredients you stock, the richer your potential variety of MMCs will be. But don't rush out and buy all the ingredients you'd need to make all 101 MMCs in this book at once. Supermarket clerks would surely look at you as though you're crazy, and you don't need that. Single out a recipe or two, and buy the required ingredients. You'll have plenty of ingredients left over to bake more MMCs.

Also, you'll want to leave some room in your grocery cart for your favorite frostings, sprinkles, jellybeans, gumdrops, fruit (fresh, frozen, and dried), and other sugary treats you can use to trim your MMCs. All of our MMC recipes include our ideas for frosting each of the mug-sized edibles, but you know best what it will take to top off your own spectacular, single-serving culinary creation as no else can. Your finishing touches let you put your personal stamp of creativity on each MMC you bake — and, once you've participated in creating the look, taste, and texture of an MMC — you own it.

So prepare to take ownership of 101 microwave mug cakes. Once you've read the MMC FAQs and GETTING STARTED, you'll be ten minutes away from a sumptuous single-serving MMC snack.

MMC FAQs

Q. What does "MMC" mean?
A. It stands for Microwave Mug Cake. Repeatedly typing, and saying, "Microwave Mug Cake" became too taxing for us after awhile, so we came up with MMC.

Q. What's the difference between an MMC and a muffin?
A. An MMC looks a lot like a muffin, and when it's fresh from the microwave oven, it tastes just as good as a warm muffin. But an MMC takes far less time, energy, and equipment to prepare than a muffin does.

Q. What type of mug should I use?
A. You need a mug that can hold 16 ounces of liquid and, to create a solid MMC that can stand on its own, we suggest that you use a mug that's shaped like a cylinder. However, you *may* use a tapered mug if you don't mind a bit of wobbling.

Q. Do I have to remove my MMC from the mug before I eat it?
A. This has been a source of heated debate among intrepid MMC testers. There are two schools of thought. The first holds that fewer dishes are better, and as long as you wait about 5 minutes for a baked MMC to cool off, you can eat it directly from the mug. The second holds that you simply can't fit enough frosting on an MMC that's trapped in a mug, and unmolding the MMC before you eat it is a must. The choice is yours. Be warned, though, that since this is such a volatile subject, it's best not to bring the topic up anyplace where the volume of the conversation can be an issue.

Q. What do I do if my microwave mug cake breaks in half while I'm removing it from the mug?
A. Use frosting to "glue" it back together again, and relax. No one will care.

Q. Do I have to use the frosting and decoration combinations that you suggest in the "fancy stuff" portion of the recipes?
A. No. The suggestions are just that. Create your own favorite frostings and decorations, or eat the microwave mug cake bare. Have it the way you like it — it's your MMC!

Q. Do I have to measure the ingredients?
A. Please do. Because it only takes a small amount of ingredients to make an MMC, the proportions matter more than in other types of baking. "Eyeballing" the orange juice and pouring in a couple of "glops" may be fine if you're making a cake. But the same glopping instead of precise measuring can cause the batter to spill over the mug and run all over your microwave. We're not trying to make your life difficult here. We're just trying to save your microwave oven — and your mug.

Q. Do I have to use a mixer and have a perfectly smooth batter?
A. No mixer is required, but do thoroughly mix the batter with a spoon or a whisk, and remove as many of the lumps as you can.

Q. Is it okay to use an egg substitute instead of an egg?
A. We'd say "no." Our intrepid MMC testers couldn't get egg substitutes to work, and they made many messes trying.

Q. What happens if I substitute, say, rye flour or buckwheat flour for all-purpose flour?
A. Try it, and let us know!

Q. How can I store an uneaten portion of the microwave mug cake for another day?
A. Don't. By the next day, you can use the leftover cake as a paperweight. Besides, you're always less than 10 minutes away from a new one. If you want to save some of your MMC for later the same day, however you can try plastic wrap (or plasticware) and hope for the best.

Q. Why do you suggest that I thump the batter-filled mug six times before baking it?
A. Because we felt that, on the seventh thump, you might break the mug. Seriously, thumping the mug firmly several times removes excess air bubbles and ensures that your finished microwave mug cake won't end up lopsided.

Q. Should I add salt to the batter?
A. No. Microwave mug cakes don't require any salt.

Q. Vanilla extract: real or imitation?
A. We'd go with the real stuff. It's more expensive, but we think that it tastes better than the artificial flavoring.

Q. What type of milk do your recipes require?
A. We use 1% milk. But it's okay to substitute other types. Soy milk and rice milk will work, too.

Q. What type of oil should I use?
A. We use canola oil, and that turns out just fine. It's okay to use your favorite cooking oil, but we'd steer clear of olive oil because of its pungent flavor.

Q. Is it okay to substitute white sugar in recipes that require light brown sugar?
A. We wouldn't, especially if you plan to eat your cake without frosting it (or to serve it to someone else). Since the microwave oven doesn't brown baked goods, the light brown sugar gives your cake a finished look.

Q. What if I run out of an ingredient?
A. You can always substitute one flavor for another flavor of the same food type. For example, you can use vanilla or tapioca pudding powder in place of pistachio pudding powder; you can swap lemon or blueberry yogurt for strawberry yogurt; or you can go with cherry or blueberry pie filling instead of lemon pie filling. In fact, making these substitutions is a great way to unleash your creativity. Try it, and let us know what you come up with!

Q. What happens if I want to get *really* creative — say, adding an extra two tablespoons of pie filling to a recipe, squirting in some pickle juice, or mixing together three different flavors of yogurt?
A. Good luck with that — and *really* get ready to thoroughly clean up your microwave oven or forfeit your mug after your experiments in the event that things go wrong. In our experience, they probably will.

Q. Is this real baking, or is it a gimmick?
A. You're using real ingredients just like any pastry chef would. You're just reducing the time and portion size.

Q. Is it selfish to bake a microwave mug cake for yourself?
A. Yes, but "selfish" isn't always a bad thing. Your loved ones want to see you happy, and if a microwave mug cake can make your day, then go for it.

Q. How hot does the mug get once the cake is baked?
A. Extremely hot. Wait two minutes before you remove the cake from the mug. And wait about five more minutes before you wash out the mug. Clean mugs are good. Burns are not.

Q. Must I use a fork to eat my MMC?
A. Not unless you sense the neighbors are watching. Finger foods can be fun.

Q. What can I use to frost my MMC?
A. In the first place, you can eat every cake "as is." But, if you want to get into the fancy stuff, you can top your cake with frosting (store bought is fine, and an unopened canister of it will last nearly forever), jelly, jam, pie filling, yogurt, or pudding (the single-serving pudding containers you buy in the supermarket are perfect, and you'll only need a couple of spoonfuls).

Q. What can I use to decorate my frosted MMC?
A. You can dust on powdered sugar or graham cracker crumbs, or you can sprinkle your frosted cake with shredded coconut, chopped nuts, small chewable candies such as gumdrops or sprinkles, or hot fudge (or your favorite flavor) sundae sauce.

Q. Stacey, you wrote the book alone. Why, then, do you refer to yourself in the first person, plural, throughout the text?
A. We don't know, but it worries us.

GETTING STARTED

It's so simple to make a Microwave Mug Cake that it's almost too easy. Many intrepid MMC testers were so excited to get started that they failed to follow our directions the first time around. One of them spent the better part of an evening cleaning out her mug (which, sadly, she hadn't greased). To ensure that your MMC-baking experiences are all good ones, please read these notes from top to bottom before you bake your first MMC.

1. Wash and dry your mug before you begin, and thoroughly grease the inside. We use cooking spray, but butter or margarine work, too.

2. Place your mug on a saucer or plate before you bake it in the microwave. That way, if the batter runs over the top of the mug, the saucer or plate will catch the spills. (Obviously, you must use a microwave-safe mug and saucer/plate.)

3. Mix the batter in a medium-sized bowl and not directly in the mug. You don't need a mixer, but you do need to thoroughly mix the ingredients. We suggest you mix the wet ingredients together first, and then add the dry ingredients.

4. Fill your mug no more than halfway with batter. While the MMC is cooking, the batter may well rise beyond the top of the mug. It will fall again before it can cause a mess in your microwave, so do not be concerned, and do not stop your microwave's cooking process prematurely.

5. Use a microwave oven with a turntable, and bake your MMC on high power for between 3 and 4 minutes. Test your MMC with a toothpick to be sure it's done.

6. Use a potholder to remove your mug from the microwave. We're crazy about the Ove Glove™, because it allows your fingers complete flexibilty and really does protect your hand.

7. Let the MMC cool for 2 minutes before you remove it from the mug. Let the mug cool for at least 5 minutes longer before you wash it.

8. Feel free to use the saucer or plate you placed under the mug to eat your unmolded MMC — provided you remembered to wash the bottom of the mug before placing it on the saucer or plate (or you have a very clean counter or table).

9. Time your MMC baking carefully. It's fine to bake yourself an MMC while you're at work when there's no one else in the break room. But, if someone

else walks in, realize that you might have to share — and be prepared to give up that which is yours in order to save a friendship or even your job.

10. Cool your MMC completely before you frost it, just as you would with a cake or muffin. Otherwise, be prepared to deal with a goopy, melted mess on your plate.

The Recipes

Amy's Juice Microwave Mug Cake

INGREDIENTS

1 egg
2 tablespoons tomato juice
1 tablespoon carrot juice
2 tablespoons oil
1/8 teaspoon vanilla extract
1/8 teaspoon baking powder
1/4 teaspoon ginger
4 tablespoons light brown sugar
2 tablespoons instant vanilla pudding
   powder (not prepared)
5 tablespoons all-purpose flour

NOTE
This juiced-up confection is named after a 23-year-old who claims it's her favorite snack. Really, Amy? What happened to those delicious carrot sticks?

DIRECTIONS

Prepare mug by coating the inside lightly with cooking spray.

Mix the ingredients in a small bowl. Beat egg first with a spoon and mix in other liquid ingredients. Then add dry ingredients and mix until you've removed all the lumps.

Pour the batter into the mug (do not fill more than halfway) and smooth the top with a spoon. Thump mug firmly on the tabletop six times to remove excess air bubbles. Place mug on top of a microwavable small plate or saucer.

Bake for 3 - 4 minutes. Check for doneness by inserting a toothpick in the middle of the microwave mug cake and removing the toothpick. If the toothpick is dry, the MMC is done.

Wait 2 minutes, then run a butter knife along the inside of the mug, and tip the cake into plate. Position the mug cake so that the slightly rounded top is on top. Your microwave mug cake will now look like a slightly overgrown muffin.

FANCY STUFF

Frost the whole Amy's Juice Microwave Mug Cake with cream cheese frosting (or just plain cream cheese), or split the MMC in half, and frost each half individually (in which case you'll end up with two separate MMCs — or you can reassemble the frosted halves to create a layered MMC). Decorate, if you wish, with powdered sugar or candied ginger.

Apple Raisin Microwave Mug Cake

INGREDIENTS

1 egg
3 tablespoons apple juice
2 tablespoons oil
1/8 teaspoon vanilla extract
1/8 teaspoon baking powder
1/4 teaspoon cinnamon
4 tablespoons sugar
2 tablespoons unsweetened
  cocoa powder
5 tablespoons all-purpose flour
2 tablespoons raisins

NOTE
Of course, you should be saving most of that apple juice to make wholesome, healthful smoothies. But just sacrifice 3 tablespoons of the juice to make yourself an Apple Raisin Microwave Mug Cake. Go ahead. You know you want it.

DIRECTIONS

Prepare mug by coating the inside lightly with cooking spray.

Mix the ingredients in a small bowl. Beat egg first with a spoon and mix in other liquid ingredients. Then add dry ingredients and mix until you've removed all the lumps.

Pour the batter into the mug (do not fill more than halfway) and smooth the top with a spoon. Thump mug firmly on the tabletop six times to remove excess air bubbles. Place mug on top of a microwavable small plate or saucer.

Bake for 3 - 4 minutes. Check for doneness by inserting a toothpick in the middle of the microwave mug cake and removing the toothpick. If the toothpick is dry, the MMC is done.

Wait 2 minutes, then run a butter knife along the inside of the mug, and tip the cake into plate. Position the mug cake so that the slightly rounded top is on top. Your microwave mug cake will now look like a slightly overgrown muffin.

FANCY STUFF

Frost the whole Apple Raisin Microwave Mug Cake with apple jelly or chocolate frosting, or split the MMC in half, and frost each half individually (in which case you'll end up with two separate MMCs — or you can reassemble the frosted halves to create a layered MMC). Decorate, if you wish, with raisins or apple slices (fresh or dried).

Apple Grapevine Microwave Mug Cake

INGREDIENTS
1 egg
3 tablespoons unsweetened
  apple juice
2 tablespoons oil
1/8 teaspoon vanilla extract
1/8 teaspoon baking powder
1/4 teaspoon cinnamon
4 tablespoons sugar
2 tablespoons unsweetened instant
  grape gelatin powder
5 tablespoons all-purpose flour

NOTE
Why do people always hear things through grapevines instead of through apple trees? Maybe it's because talking to an apple tree is like talking to wood.

DIRECTIONS
Prepare mug by coating the inside lightly with cooking spray.

Mix the ingredients in a small bowl. Beat egg first with a spoon and mix in other liquid ingredients. Then add dry ingredients and mix until you've removed all the lumps.

Pour the batter into the mug (do not fill more than halfway) and smooth the top with a spoon. Thump mug firmly on the tabletop six times to remove excess air bubbles. Place mug on top of a microwavable small plate or saucer.

Bake for 3 - 4 minutes. Check for doneness by inserting a toothpick in the middle of the microwave mug cake and removing the toothpick. If the toothpick is dry, the MMC is done.

Wait 2 minutes, then run a butter knife along the inside of the mug, and tip the cake into plate. Position the mug cake so that the slightly rounded top is on top. Your microwave mug cake will now look like a slightly overgrown muffin.

FANCY STUFF
Frost the whole Apple Grapevine Microwave Mug Cake with apple or grape jelly, or split the MMC in half, and frost each half individually (in which case you'll end up with two separate MMCs — or you can reassemble the frosted halves to create a layered MMC). Decorate, if you wish, with powdered sugar, or with apples slices (fresh or dried).

Aprilla Microwave Mug Cake

INGREDIENTS

1 egg
1 tablespoon apricot baby food
1 tablespoon oil
1/8 teaspoon vanilla extract
1/8 teaspoon baking powder
1/4 teaspoon cinnamon
4 tablespoons light brown sugar
2 tablespoons instant vanilla
  pudding powder (not prepared)
4 tablespoons all-purpose flour

NOTE
Who among us is too mature or jaded to enjoy the fresh-picked quality of the apricot baby food from our childhoods? Let's see a show of hands, please. Anyone?

DIRECTIONS

Prepare mug by coating the inside lightly with cooking spray.

Mix the ingredients in a small bowl. Beat egg first with a spoon and mix in other liquid ingredients. Then add dry ingredients and mix until you've removed all the lumps.

Pour the batter into the mug (do not fill more than halfway) and smooth the top with a spoon. Thump mug firmly on the tabletop six times to remove excess air bubbles. Place mug on top of a microwavable small plate or saucer.

Bake for 3 - 4 minutes. Check for doneness by inserting a toothpick in the middle of the microwave mug cake and removing the toothpick. If the toothpick is dry, the MMC is done.

Wait 2 minutes, then run a butter knife along the inside of the mug, and tip the cake into plate. Position the mug cake so that the slightly rounded top is on top. Your microwave mug cake will now look like a slightly overgrown muffin.

FANCY STUFF

Frost the whole Aprilla Microwave Mug Cake with apricot jelly, or split the MMC in half, and frost each half individually (in which case you'll end up with two separate MMCs — or you can reassemble the frosted halves to create a layered MMC). Decorate, if you wish, with powdered sugar or apricot slices (fresh or dried).

Baked Apple Vanilla Microwave Mug Cake

INGREDIENTS
1 egg
1 tablespoon apple sauce
1 tablespoon oil
1/8 teaspoon vanilla extract
1/8 teaspoon baking powder
1/4 teaspoon cinnamon
4 tablespoons light brown sugar
2 tablespoons instant vanilla
   pudding powder (not prepared)
4 tablespoons all-purpose flour

NOTE
Nine out of ten apples surveyed prefer to be nuked in the microwave rather than to be baked in the oven. Then again, those nine apples also admit to regularly visiting tanning salons.

DIRECTIONS
Prepare mug by coating the inside lightly with cooking spray.

Mix the ingredients in a small bowl. Beat egg first with a spoon and mix in other liquid ingredients. Then add dry ingredients and mix until you've removed all the lumps.

Pour the batter into the mug (do not fill more than halfway) and smooth the top with a spoon. Thump mug firmly on the tabletop six times to remove excess air bubbles. Place mug on top of a microwavable small plate or saucer.

Bake for 3 - 4 minutes. Check for doneness by inserting a toothpick in the middle of the microwave mug cake and removing the toothpick. If the toothpick is dry, the MMC is done.

Wait 2 minutes, then run a butter knife along the inside of the mug, and tip the cake into plate. Position the mug cake so that the slightly rounded top is on top. Your microwave mug cake will now look like a slightly overgrown muffin.

FANCY STUFF
Frost the whole Baked Apple Vanilla Microwave Mug Cake with vanilla frosting, or split the MMC in half, and frost each half individually (in which case you'll end up with two separate MMCs — or you can reassemble the frosted halves to create a layered MMC). Decorate, if you wish, with apples slices (fresh or dried).

Banana Nana Microwave Mug Cake

INGREDIENTS
1 egg
1 tablespoon banana baby food
1 tablespoon oil
1/8 teaspoon vanilla extract
1/8 teaspoon baking powder
1/4 teaspoon ginger
1/4 teaspoon cinnamon
4 tablespoons light brown sugar
2 tablespoons instant banana
   pudding powder (not prepared)
4 tablespoons all-purpose flour

NOTE
Is there any such thing as too much banana flavor? Not according to the chimps we surveyed.

DIRECTIONS
Prepare mug by coating the inside lightly with cooking spray.

Mix the ingredients in a small bowl. Beat egg first with a spoon and mix in other liquid ingredients. Then add dry ingredients and mix until you've removed all the lumps.

Pour the batter into the mug (do not fill more than halfway) and smooth the top with a spoon. Thump mug firmly on the tabletop six times to remove excess air bubbles. Place mug on top of a microwavable small plate or saucer.

Bake for 3 - 4 minutes. Check for doneness by inserting a toothpick in the middle of the microwave mug cake and removing the toothpick. If the toothpick is dry, the MMC is done.

Wait 2 minutes, then run a butter knife along the inside of the mug, and tip the cake into plate. Position the mug cake so that the slightly rounded top is on top. Your microwave mug cake will now look like a slightly overgrown muffin.

FANCY STUFF
Frost the whole Banana Nana Microwave Mug Cake with banana pudding or banana yogurt, or split the MMC in half, and frost each half individually (in which case you'll end up with two separate MMCs — or you can reassemble the frosted halves to create a layered MMC). Decorate, if you wish, with banana slices (fresh or dried).

Bananacot Microwave Mug Cake

INGREDIENTS
1 egg
1 tablespoon apricot baby food
1 tablespoon oil
1/8 teaspoon vanilla extract
1/8 teaspoon baking powder
1/4 teaspoon cinnamon
4 tablespoons light brown sugar
2 tablespoons instant banana
   pudding powder (not prepared)
4 tablespoons all-purpose flour

NOTE
Just close your eyes for a moment, and imagine you're on a tropical island with rows of bananacot trees swaying in the breeze. Okay. Now imagine there's a hurricane coming, and everyone has to run into a cave and hide. Sort of spoils everything, doesn't it?

DIRECTIONS
Prepare mug by coating the inside lightly with cooking spray.

Mix the ingredients in a small bowl. Beat egg first with a spoon and mix in other liquid ingredients. Then add dry ingredients and mix until you've removed all the lumps.

Pour the batter into the mug (do not fill more than halfway) and smooth the top with a spoon. Thump mug firmly on the tabletop six times to remove excess air bubbles. Place mug on top of a microwavable small plate or saucer.

Bake for 3 - 4 minutes. Check for doneness by inserting a toothpick in the middle of the microwave mug cake and removing the toothpick. If the toothpick is dry, the MMC is done.

Wait 2 minutes, then run a butter knife along the inside of the mug, and tip the cake into plate. Position the mug cake so that the slightly rounded top is on top. Your microwave mug cake will now look like a slightly overgrown muffin.

FANCY STUFF
Frost the whole Bananacot Microwave Mug Cake with prepared banana pudding or banana yogurt, or split the MMC in half, and frost each half individually (in which case you'll end up with two separate MMCs — or you can reassemble the frosted halves to create a layered MMC). Decorate, if you wish, with banana or apricot slices (fresh or dried).

Berry Patch Microwave Mug Cake

INGREDIENTS

1 egg
1 tablespoon blueberry pie filling
2 tablespoons oil
1/8 teaspoon vanilla extract
1/8 teaspoon baking powder
4 tablespoons sugar
2 tablespoons strawberry-flavored
  NESQUIK®
4 tablespoons all-purpose flour

NOTE
Civilization may have reached its peak when berries migrated from bushes and plants to canned pie fillings and powdered drink mixes. It's sort of like when primitive fish migrated from ancient oceans into seafood restaurants.

DIRECTIONS

Prepare mug by coating the inside lightly with cooking spray.

Mix the ingredients in a small bowl. Beat egg first with a spoon and mix in other liquid ingredients. Then add dry ingredients and mix until you've removed all the lumps.

Pour the batter into the mug (do not fill more than halfway) and smooth the top with a spoon. Thump mug firmly on the tabletop six times to remove excess air bubbles. Place mug on top of a microwavable small plate or saucer.

Bake for 3 - 4 minutes. Check for doneness by inserting a toothpick in the middle of the microwave mug cake and removing the toothpick. If the toothpick is dry, the MMC is done.

Wait 2 minutes, then run a butter knife along the inside of the mug, and tip the cake into plate. Position the mug cake so that the slightly rounded top is on top. Your microwave mug cake will now look like a slightly overgrown muffin.

FANCY STUFF

Frost the whole Berry Patch Microwave Mug Cake with blueberry pie filling, or split the MMC in half, and frost each half individually (in which case you'll end up with two separate MMCs — or you can reassemble the frosted halves to create a layered MMC). Decorate, if you wish, with fresh or frozen blueberries or strawberry slices.

Black Forest Microwave Mug Cake

INGREDIENTS

1 egg
1 tablespoon cherry pie filling
1 tablespoon oil
1/8 teaspoon vanilla extract
1/8 teaspoon baking powder
1/4 teaspoon cinnamon
4 tablespoons sugar
2 tablespoons unsweetened
  cocoa powder
4 tablespoons all-purpose flour

NOTE

What color does a "black forest" turn in springtime? None of the cherries or cocoa beans we asked had a clue. Either that, or they just weren't telling us.

DIRECTIONS

Prepare mug by coating the inside lightly with cooking spray.

Mix the ingredients in a small bowl. Beat egg first with a spoon and mix in other liquid ingredients. Then add dry ingredients and mix until you've removed all the lumps.

Pour the batter into the mug (do not fill more than halfway) and smooth the top with a spoon. Thump mug firmly on the tabletop six times to remove excess air bubbles. Place mug on top of a microwavable small plate or saucer.

Bake for 3 - 4 minutes. Check for doneness by inserting a toothpick in the middle of the microwave mug cake and removing the toothpick. If the toothpick is dry, the MMC is done.

Wait 2 minutes, then run a butter knife along the inside of the mug, and tip the cake into plate. Position the mug cake so that the slightly rounded top is on top. Your microwave mug cake will now look like a slightly overgrown muffin.

FANCY STUFF

Frost the whole Black Forest Microwave Mug Cake with cherry pie filling, or split the MMC in half, and frost each half individually (in which case you'll end up with two separate MMCs — or you can reassemble the frosted halves to create a layered MMC). Decorate, if you wish, with cherries.

Blueberry Muffin Microwave Mug Cake

INGREDIENTS

1 egg

2 tablespoons mixed blueberry
   yogurt (with the fruit stirred in)

1 tablespoon oil

1/8 teaspoon vanilla extract

1/8 teaspoon baking powder

1/4 teaspoon cinnamon

4 tablespoons light brown sugar

2 tablespoons instant vanilla
   pudding powder (not prepared)

4 tablespoons all-purpose flour

NOTE

Once upon a time, there was a department store in Boston called Jordan Marsh that sold the best blueberry muffins on the entire planet. They tasted nothing like the Blueberry Muffin Microwave Mug Cake. We're just saying....

DIRECTIONS

Prepare mug by coating the inside lightly with cooking spray.

Mix the ingredients in a small bowl. Beat egg first with a spoon and mix in other liquid ingredients. Then add dry ingredients and mix until you've removed all the lumps.

Pour the batter into the mug (do not fill more than halfway) and smooth the top with a spoon. Thump mug firmly on the tabletop six times to remove excess air bubbles. Place mug on top of a microwavable small plate or saucer.

Bake for 3 - 4 minutes. Check for doneness by inserting a toothpick in the middle of the microwave mug cake and removing the toothpick. If the toothpick is dry, the MMC is done.

Wait 2 minutes, then run a butter knife along the inside of the mug, and tip the cake into plate. Position the mug cake so that the slightly rounded top is on top. Your microwave mug cake will now look like a slightly overgrown muffin.

FANCY STUFF

Frost the whole Blueberry Muffin Microwave Mug Cake with blueberry pie filling, blueberry jelly, or the rest of the blueberry yogurt, or split the MMC in half, and frost each half individually (in which case you'll end up with two separate MMCs — or you can reassemble the frosted halves to create a layered MMC). Decorate, if you wish, with fresh or frozen blueberries.

Butterscotch Banana Microwave Mug Cake

INGREDIENTS
1 egg
1 tablespoon butterscotch
  pudding (prepared)
2 tablespoons oil
1/8 teaspoon vanilla extract
1/8 teaspoon baking powder
1/4 teaspoon cinnamon
4 tablespoons light brown sugar
2 tablespoons instant banana
  pudding powder (not prepared)
4 tablespoons all-purpose flour

NOTE
Why does the banana play second banana to the butterscotch in the Butterscotch Banana Microwave Mug Cake? And what does that make the butterscotch — the first banana?

DIRECTIONS
Prepare mug by coating the inside lightly with cooking spray.

Mix the ingredients in a small bowl. Beat egg first with a spoon and mix in other liquid ingredients. Then add dry ingredients and mix until you've removed all the lumps.

Pour the batter into the mug (do not fill more than halfway) and smooth the top with a spoon. Thump mug firmly on the tabletop six times to remove excess air bubbles. Place mug on top of a microwavable small plate or saucer.

Bake for 3 - 4 minutes. Check for doneness by inserting a toothpick in the middle of the microwave mug cake and removing the toothpick. If the toothpick is dry, the MMC is done.

Wait 2 minutes, then run a butter knife along the inside of the mug, and tip the cake into plate. Position the mug cake so that the slightly rounded top is on top. Your microwave mug cake will now look like a slightly overgrown muffin.

FANCY STUFF
Frost the whole Butterscotch Banana Microwave Mug Cake with prepared banana pudding, or split the MMC in half, and frost each half individually (in which case you'll end up with two separate MMCs — or you can reassemble the frosted halves to create a layered MMC). Decorate, if you wish, with butterscotch chips.

Butterscotch Caramel Microwave Mug Cake

INGREDIENTS

1 egg
1 tablespoon caramel sundae syrup
1 tablespoon oil
1/8 teaspoon vanilla extract
1/8 teaspoon baking powder
1/4 teaspoon cinnamon
4 tablespoons light brown sugar
2 tablespoons instant butterscotch pudding powder (not prepared)
4 tablespoons all-purpose flour

NOTE
One of our intrepid MMC testers came up with the idea for the Butterscotch Caramel Microwave Mug Cake. Her dentist loved the idea.

DIRECTIONS

Prepare mug by coating the inside lightly with cooking spray.

Mix the ingredients in a small bowl. Beat egg first with a spoon and mix in other liquid ingredients. Then add dry ingredients and mix until you've removed all the lumps.

Pour the batter into the mug (do not fill more than halfway) and smooth the top with a spoon. Thump mug firmly on the tabletop six times to remove excess air bubbles. Place mug on top of a microwavable small plate or saucer.

Bake for 3 - 4 minutes. Check for doneness by inserting a toothpick in the middle of the microwave mug cake and removing the toothpick. If the toothpick is dry, the MMC is done.

Wait 2 minutes, then run a butter knife along the inside of the mug, and tip the cake into plate. Position the mug cake so that the slightly rounded top is on top. Your microwave mug cake will now look like a slightly overgrown muffin.

FANCY STUFF

Frost the whole Butterscotch Caramel Microwave Mug Cake with prepared butterscotch pudding, or split the MMC in half, and frost each half individually (in which case you'll end up with two separate MMCs — or you can reassemble the frosted halves to create a layered MMC). Decorate, if you wish, with caramel syrup.

Butterscotch Coconut Cream Microwave Mug Cake

INGREDIENTS

1 egg
1 tablespoon butterscotch
pudding (prepared)
2 tablespoons oil
1/8 teaspoon vanilla extract
1/8 teaspoon baking powder
1/4 teaspoon cinnamon
4 tablespoons light brown sugar
2 tablespoons coconut cream instant
pudding powder (not prepared)
4 tablespoons all-purpose flour

NOTE

It's too bad they wasted so many coconuts making those old jungle movies, because if they hadn't, just think how much more coconut cream pudding there'd be in the world.

DIRECTIONS

Prepare mug by coating the inside lightly with cooking spray.

Mix the ingredients in a small bowl. Beat egg first with a spoon and mix in other liquid ingredients. Then add dry ingredients and mix until you've removed all the lumps.

Pour the batter into the mug (do not fill more than halfway) and smooth the top with a spoon. Thump mug firmly on the tabletop six times to remove excess air bubbles. Place mug on top of a microwavable small plate or saucer.

Bake for 3 - 4 minutes. Check for doneness by inserting a toothpick in the middle of the microwave mug cake and removing the toothpick. If the toothpick is dry, the MMC is done.

Wait 2 minutes, then run a butter knife along the inside of the mug, and tip the cake into plate. Position the mug cake so that the slightly rounded top is on top. Your microwave mug cake will now look like a slightly overgrown muffin.

FANCY STUFF

Frost the whole Butterscotch Coconut Cream Microwave Mug Cake with prepared butterscotch pudding, or split the MMC in half, and frost each half individually (in which case you'll end up with two separate MMCs — or you can reassemble the frosted halves to create a layered MMC). Decorate, if you wish, with shredded coconut.

Butterstrawberry Chip Microwave Mug Cake

INGREDIENTS
1 egg
3 tablespoons milk
3 tablespoons oil
1/8 teaspoon vanilla extract
1/8 teaspoon baking powder
1/4 teaspoon cinnamon
4 tablespoons light brown sugar
1 tablespoon strawberry-flavored
  NESQUIK®
1 tablespoon instant butterscotch
  pudding powder (not prepared)
4 tablespoons all-purpose flour
2 tablespoons butterscotch chips

NOTE
If there actually were butterstrawberry chips, could they put potato chips out of business?

DIRECTIONS
Prepare mug by coating the inside lightly with cooking spray.

Mix the ingredients in a small bowl. Beat egg first with a spoon and mix in other liquid ingredients. Then add dry ingredients and mix until you've removed all the lumps.

Pour the batter into the mug (do not fill more than halfway) and smooth the top with a spoon. Thump mug firmly on the tabletop six times to remove excess air bubbles. Place mug on top of a microwavable small plate or saucer.

Bake for 3 - 4 minutes. Check for doneness by inserting a toothpick in the middle of the microwave mug cake and removing the toothpick. If the toothpick is dry, the MMC is done.

Wait 2 minutes, then run a butter knife along the inside of the mug, and tip the cake into plate. Position the mug cake so that the slightly rounded top is on top. Your microwave mug cake will now look like a slightly overgrown muffin.

FANCY STUFF
Frost the whole Butterstrawberry Chip Microwave Mug Cake with strawberry jelly or your favorite frosting, or split the MMC in half, and frost each half individually (in which case you'll end up with two separate MMCs — or you can reassemble the frosted halves to create a layered MMC). Decorate, if you wish, with butterscotch chips.

Carrot Spice Microwave Mug Cake

INGREDIENTS
1 egg
1 tablespoon carrot baby food
1 tablespoon oil
1/8 teaspoon vanilla extract
1/8 teaspoon baking powder
1/4 teaspoon cinnamon
4 tablespoons light brown sugar
2 tablespoons instant vanilla
   pudding powder (not prepared)
4 tablespoons all-purpose flour

NOTE
How many years must a cartoon character bunny work before he or she can retire and collect Social Security payments? We wanted to find out, but none of the cartoon character bunnies we contacted would return our phone calls.

DIRECTIONS
Prepare mug by coating the inside lightly with cooking spray.

Mix the ingredients in a small bowl. Beat egg first with a spoon and mix in other liquid ingredients. Then add dry ingredients and mix until you've removed all the lumps.

Pour the batter into the mug (do not fill more than halfway) and smooth the top with a spoon. Thump mug firmly on the tabletop six times to remove excess air bubbles. Place mug on top of a microwavable small plate or saucer.

Bake for 3 - 4 minutes. Check for doneness by inserting a toothpick in the middle of the microwave mug cake and removing the toothpick. If the toothpick is dry, the MMC is done.

Wait 2 minutes, then run a butter knife along the inside of the mug, and tip the cake into plate. Position the mug cake so that the slightly rounded top is on top. Your microwave mug cake will now look like a slightly overgrown muffin.

FANCY STUFF
Frost the whole Carrot Spice Microwave Mug Cake with cream cheese frosting or just plain cream cheese, or split the MMC in half, and frost each half individually (in which case you'll end up with two separate MMCs — or you can reassemble the frosted halves to create a layered MMC). Decorate, if you wish, with cinnamon.

Cherranilla Microwave Mug Cake

INGREDIENTS

1 egg
1 tablespoon cherry pie filling
1 tablespoon oil
1/8 teaspoon vanilla extract
1/8 teaspoon baking powder
1/4 teaspoon cinnamon
4 tablespoons light brown sugar
2 tablespoons instant vanilla
pudding powder (not prepared)
4 tablespoons all-purpose flour

NOTE
Cherranilla may sound like a big, scary spider, but it's actually the name of the spider's lawyer.

DIRECTIONS

Prepare mug by coating the inside lightly with cooking spray.

Mix the ingredients in a small bowl. Beat egg first with a spoon and mix in other liquid ingredients. Then add dry ingredients and mix until you've removed all the lumps.

Pour the batter into the mug (do not fill more than halfway) and smooth the top with a spoon. Thump mug firmly on the tabletop six times to remove excess air bubbles. Place mug on top of a microwavable small plate or saucer.

Bake for 3 - 4 minutes. Check for doneness by inserting a toothpick in the middle of the microwave mug cake and removing the toothpick. If the toothpick is dry, the MMC is done.

Wait 2 minutes, then run a butter knife along the inside of the mug, and tip the cake into plate. Position the mug cake so that the slightly rounded top is on top. Your microwave mug cake will now look like a slightly overgrown muffin.

FANCY STUFF

Frost the whole Cherranilla Microwave Mug Cake with cherry pie filling, or split the MMC in half, and frost each half individually (in which case you'll end up with two separate MMCs — or you can reassemble the frosted halves to create a layered MMC). Decorate, if you wish, with cherries.

Cherry Cheesecake Microwave Mug Cake

INGREDIENTS

1 egg
**1 tablespoon softened
   cream cheese**
1 tablespoon ricotta cheese
2 tablespoons oil
1/8 teaspoon vanilla extract
1/8 teaspoon baking powder
1/4 teaspoon cinnamon
4 tablespoons light brown sugar
**2 tablespoons cherry instant
   gelatin powder (not prepared)**
1 tablespoon graham cracker crumbs
4 tablespoons all-purpose flour

NOTE
*Why is "ricotta" cheese so much
more fun to say than "cream"
cheese?*

DIRECTIONS

Prepare mug by coating the inside lightly with cooking spray.

Mix the ingredients in a small bowl. Beat egg first with a spoon and mix
in other liquid ingredients. Then add dry ingredients and mix until you've
removed all the lumps.

Pour the batter into the mug (do not fill more than halfway) and smooth the
top with a spoon. Thump mug firmly on the tabletop six times to remove
excess air bubbles. Place mug on top of a microwavable small plate or saucer.

Bake for 3 - 4 minutes. Check for doneness by inserting a toothpick in the
middle of the microwave mug cake and removing the toothpick. If the
toothpick is dry, the MMC is done.

Wait 2 minutes, then run a butter knife along the inside of the mug, and tip
the cake into plate. Position the mug cake so that the slightly rounded top
is on top. Your microwave mug cake will now look like a slightly overgrown
muffin.

FANCY STUFF

Frost the whole Cherry Cheesecake Microwave Mug Cake with cherry pie
filling, or split the MMC in half, and frost each half individually (in which case
you'll end up with two separate MMCs — or you can reassemble the frosted
halves to create a layered MMC). Decorate, if you wish, with graham cracker
crumbs or cherries.

Cherry Lemon Microwave Mug Cake

INGREDIENTS
1 egg
2 tablespoons lemon yogurt
1 tablespoon oil
1/8 teaspoon vanilla extract
1/8 teaspoon baking powder
1/4 teaspoon cinnamon
4 tablespoons light brown sugar
**2 tablespoons instant cherry
  pudding powder (not prepared)**
4 tablespoons all-purpose flour

NOTE
*The Cherry Lemon Microwave
Mug Cake — doesn't it sound sort
of like a slot machine?*

DIRECTIONS
Prepare mug by coating the inside lightly with cooking spray.

Mix the ingredients in a small bowl. Beat egg first with a spoon and mix
in other liquid ingredients. Then add dry ingredients and mix until you've
removed all the lumps.

Pour the batter into the mug (do not fill more than halfway) and smooth the
top with a spoon. Thump mug firmly on the tabletop six times to remove
excess air bubbles. Place mug on top of a microwavable small plate or saucer.

Bake for 3 - 4 minutes. Check for doneness by inserting a toothpick in the
middle of the microwave mug cake and removing the toothpick. If the
toothpick is dry, the MMC is done.

Wait 2 minutes, then run a butter knife along the inside of the mug, and tip
the cake into plate. Position the mug cake so that the slightly rounded top
is on top. Your microwave mug cake will now look like a slightly overgrown
muffin.

FANCY STUFF
Frost the whole Cherry Lemon Microwave Mug Cake with cherry or lemon
pie filling, or split the MMC in half, and frost each half individually (in which
case you'll end up with two separate MMCs — or you can reassemble the
frosted halves to create a layered MMC). Decorate, if you wish, with cherries.

Cherry Pineapple Microwave Mug Cake

INGREDIENTS
1 egg
2 tablespoons pineapple yogurt
(with the fruit stirred in)
1 tablespoon oil
1/8 teaspoon vanilla extract
1/8 teaspoon baking powder
1/4 teaspoon cinnamon
4 tablespoons light brown sugar
2 tablespoons instant cherry
pudding powder (not prepared)
4 tablespoons all-purpose flour

NOTE
What did the cherry say to the pineapple? We don't know. The pineapple didn't tell us.

DIRECTIONS
Prepare mug by coating the inside lightly with cooking spray.

Mix the ingredients in a small bowl. Beat egg first with a spoon and mix in other liquid ingredients. Then add dry ingredients and mix until you've removed all the lumps.

Pour the batter into the mug (do not fill more than halfway) and smooth the top with a spoon. Thump mug firmly on the tabletop six times to remove excess air bubbles. Place mug on top of a microwavable small plate or saucer.

Bake for 3 - 4 minutes. Check for doneness by inserting a toothpick in the middle of the microwave mug cake and removing the toothpick. If the toothpick is dry, the MMC is done.

Wait 2 minutes, then run a butter knife along the inside of the mug, and tip the cake into plate. Position the mug cake so that the slightly rounded top is on top. Your microwave mug cake will now look like a slightly overgrown muffin.

FANCY STUFF
Frost the whole Cherry Pineapple Microwave Mug Cake with pineapple yogurt, or split the MMC in half, and frost each half individually (in which case you'll end up with two separate MMCs — or you can reassemble the frosted halves to create a layered MMC). Decorate, if you wish, with cherries or pineapple chunks.

Cherry Pomegranate Microwave Mug Cake

INGREDIENTS

1 egg
2 tablespoons cherry yogurt
 (with the fruit stirred in)
1 tablespoon oil
1/8 teaspoon vanilla extract
1/8 teaspoon baking powder
1/4 teaspoon cinnamon
4 tablespoons light brown sugar
1 tablespoon Cherry Pomegranate
 Crystal Light powder
 (that's one individual package)
5 tablespoons all-purpose flour
2 tablespoons dried cranberries

NOTE

A little bit of fun has gone out of the cherry and the pomegranate now we know they're good for us. That's why we had to build an MMC around them. It just makes us feel better.

DIRECTIONS

Prepare mug by coating the inside lightly with cooking spray.

Mix the ingredients in a small bowl. Beat egg first with a spoon and mix in other liquid ingredients. Then add dry ingredients and mix until you've removed all the lumps.

Pour the batter into the mug (do not fill more than halfway) and smooth the top with a spoon. Thump mug firmly on the tabletop six times to remove excess air bubbles. Place mug on top of a microwavable small plate or saucer.

Bake for 3 - 4 minutes. Check for doneness by inserting a toothpick in the middle of the microwave mug cake and removing the toothpick. If the toothpick is dry, the MMC is done.

Wait 2 minutes, then run a butter knife along the inside of the mug, and tip the cake into plate. Position the mug cake so that the slightly rounded top is on top. Your microwave mug cake will now look like a slightly overgrown muffin.

FANCY STUFF

Frost the whole Cherry Pomegranate Microwave Mug Cake with cherry pie filling or the rest of the cherry yogurt, or split the MMC in half, and frost each half individually (in which case you'll end up with two separate MMCs — or you can reassemble the frosted halves to create a layered MMC). Decorate, if you wish, with cherries.

Chocoberry Microwave Mug Cake

INGREDIENTS
1 egg
2 tablespoons raspberry yogurt
(with the fruit stirred in)
1 tablespoon oil
1/8 teaspoon vanilla extract
1/8 teaspoon baking powder
4 tablespoons sugar
2 tablespoons unsweetened
cocoa powder
4 tablespoons all-purpose flour

NOTE
If the word "chocoberry" brings to mind a sugary cereal that you grew up eating in the morning, then you probably had a very scary childhood, indeed, and helping you is probably beyond the scope of this book. See our sequel.

DIRECTIONS
Prepare mug by coating the inside lightly with cooking spray.

Mix the ingredients in a small bowl. Beat egg first with a spoon and mix in other liquid ingredients. Then add dry ingredients and mix until you've removed all the lumps.

Pour the batter into the mug (do not fill more than halfway) and smooth the top with a spoon. Thump mug firmly on the tabletop six times to remove excess air bubbles. Place mug on top of a microwavable small plate or saucer.

Bake for 3 - 4 minutes. Check for doneness by inserting a toothpick in the middle of the microwave mug cake and removing the toothpick. If the toothpick is dry, the MMC is done.

Wait 2 minutes, then run a butter knife along the inside of the mug, and tip the cake into plate. Position the mug cake so that the slightly rounded top is on top. Your microwave mug cake will now look like a slightly overgrown muffin.

FANCY STUFF
Frost the whole Chocoberry Microwave Mug Cake with raspberry yogurt, or split the MMC in half, and frost each half individually (in which case you'll end up with two separate MMCs — or you can reassemble the frosted halves to create a layered MMC). Decorate, if you wish, with fresh or frozen raspberries.

Chocolate and Butterscotch Microwave Mug Cake

INGREDIENTS

1 egg
3 tablespoons milk
3 tablespoons oil
1/8 teaspoon vanilla extract
1/8 teaspoon baking powder
4 tablespoons sugar
1 tablespoon instant butterscotch
  pudding powder (not prepared)
1 tablespoon unsweetened
  cocoa powder
4 tablespoons all-purpose flour

NOTE
Why don't we ever hear of a war between chocolate and butterscotch? We can all learn from them.

DIRECTIONS

Prepare mug by coating the inside lightly with cooking spray.

Mix the ingredients in a small bowl. Beat egg first with a spoon and mix in other liquid ingredients. Then add dry ingredients and mix until you've removed all the lumps.

Pour the batter into the mug (do not fill more than halfway) and smooth the top with a spoon. Thump mug firmly on the tabletop six times to remove excess air bubbles. Place mug on top of a microwavable small plate or saucer.

Bake for 3 - 4 minutes. Check for doneness by inserting a toothpick in the middle of the microwave mug cake and removing the toothpick. If the toothpick is dry, the MMC is done.

Wait 2 minutes, then run a butter knife along the inside of the mug, and tip the cake into plate. Position the mug cake so that the slightly rounded top is on top. Your microwave mug cake will now look like a slightly overgrown muffin.

FANCY STUFF

Frost the whole Chocolate and Butterscotch Microwave Mug Cake with prepared chocolate frosting, or split the MMC in half, and frost each half individually (in which case you'll end up with two separate MMCs — or you can reassemble the frosted halves to create a layered MMC). Decorate, if you wish, with semi-sweet chocolate or butterscotch chips.

Chocolate Blueberry Microwave Mug Cake

INGREDIENTS

1 egg
1 tablespoon blueberry pie filling
2 tablespoons oil
1/8 teaspoon vanilla extract
1/8 teaspoon baking powder
4 tablespoons sugar
2 tablespoons unsweetened
  cocoa powder
4 tablespoons all-purpose flour

NOTE
If you've never had an opportunity go and pick yourself a pail full of fresh, wild blueberries, then the Chocolate Blueberry Microwave Mug Cake won't help one bit.

DIRECTIONS

Prepare mug by coating the inside lightly with cooking spray.

Mix the ingredients in a small bowl. Beat egg first with a spoon and mix in other liquid ingredients. Then add dry ingredients and mix until you've removed all the lumps.

Pour the batter into the mug (do not fill more than halfway) and smooth the top with a spoon. Thump mug firmly on the tabletop six times to remove excess air bubbles. Place mug on top of a microwavable small plate or saucer.

Bake for 3 - 4 minutes. Check for doneness by inserting a toothpick in the middle of the microwave mug cake and removing the toothpick. If the toothpick is dry, the MMC is done.

Wait 2 minutes, then run a butter knife along the inside of the mug, and tip the cake into plate. Position the mug cake so that the slightly rounded top is on top. Your microwave mug cake will now look like a slightly overgrown muffin.

FANCY STUFF

Frost the whole Chocolate Blueberry Microwave Mug Cake with blueberry pie filling, or split the MMC in half, and frost each half individually (in which case you'll end up with two separate MMCs — or you can reassemble the frosted halves to create a layered MMC). Decorate, if you wish, with small candies, or with fresh or frozen blueberries.

Chocolate Caramel Microwave Mug Cake

INGREDIENTS
1 egg
1 tablespoon caramel sundae syrup
1 tablespoon oil
1/8 teaspoon vanilla extract
1/8 teaspoon baking powder
4 tablespoons sugar
**2 tablespoons unsweetened
  cocoa powder**
4 tablespoons all-purpose flour

NOTE
*Can you really call it "chocolate
caramel" if you don't have to pick
gobs of it out of your teeth?*

DIRECTIONS
Prepare mug by coating the inside lightly with cooking spray.

Mix the ingredients in a small bowl. Beat egg first with a spoon and mix
in other liquid ingredients. Then add dry ingredients and mix until you've
removed all the lumps.

Pour the batter into the mug (do not fill more than halfway) and smooth the
top with a spoon. Thump mug firmly on the tabletop six times to remove
excess air bubbles. Place mug on top of a microwavable small plate or saucer.

Bake for 3 - 4 minutes. Check for doneness by inserting a toothpick in the
middle of the microwave mug cake and removing the toothpick. If the
toothpick is dry, the MMC is done.

Wait 2 minutes, then run a butter knife along the inside of the mug, and tip
the cake into plate. Position the mug cake so that the slightly rounded top
is on top. Your microwave mug cake will now look like a slightly overgrown
muffin.

FANCY STUFF
Frost the whole Chocolate Caramel Microwave Mug Cake with chocolate
frosting, or split the MMC in half, and frost each half individually (in which
case you'll end up with two separate MMCs — or you can reassemble the
frosted halves to create a layered MMC). Decorate, if you wish, with caramel
sundae syrup.

Chocolate Cheesecake Microwave Mug Cake

INGREDIENTS
1 egg
1 tablespoon softened cream cheese
1 tablespoon ricotta cheese
2 tablespoons oil
1/8 teaspoon vanilla extract
1/8 teaspoon baking powder
1/4 teaspoon cinnamon
4 tablespoons light brown sugar
2 tablespoons unsweetened
  cocoa powder
1 tablespoon graham cracker crumbs
4 tablespoons all-purpose flour

NOTE
*Can you think of a better job
than to work in a cheesecake
factory? Well, maybe working in
a microwave mug cake factory
would be nearly as much fun!*

DIRECTIONS
Prepare mug by coating the inside lightly with cooking spray.

Mix the ingredients in a small bowl. Beat egg first with a spoon and mix
in other liquid ingredients. Then add dry ingredients and mix until you've
removed all the lumps.

Pour the batter into the mug (do not fill more than halfway) and smooth the
top with a spoon. Thump mug firmly on the tabletop six times to remove
excess air bubbles. Place mug on top of a microwavable small plate or saucer.

Bake for 3 - 4 minutes. Check for doneness by inserting a toothpick in the
middle of the microwave mug cake and removing the toothpick. If the
toothpick is dry, the MMC is done.

Wait 2 minutes, then run a butter knife along the inside of the mug, and tip
the cake into plate. Position the mug cake so that the slightly rounded top
is on top. Your microwave mug cake will now look like a slightly overgrown
muffin.

FANCY STUFF
Frost the whole Chocolate Cheesecake Microwave Mug Cake
with chocolate frosting, or split the MMC in half, and frost each half
individually (in which case you'll end up with two separate
MMCs — or you can reassemble the frosted halves to create a layered MMC).
Decorate, if you wish, with graham cracker crumbs.

Chocolate Chip Butterscotch Microwave Mug Cake

INGREDIENTS

1 egg
3 tablespoons milk
3 tablespoons oil
1/8 teaspoon vanilla extract
1/8 teaspoon baking powder
1/4 teaspoon cinnamon
4 tablespoons light brown sugar
2 tablespoons instant butterscotch
   pudding powder (not prepared)
4 tablespoons all-purpose flour
2 tablespoons semi-sweet chocolate chips

NOTE
You don't see too many people eating raw MMC dough, even if it does have chocolate chips in it. That's strange.

DIRECTIONS

Prepare mug by coating the inside lightly with cooking spray.

Mix the ingredients in a small bowl. Beat egg first with a spoon and mix in other liquid ingredients. Then add dry ingredients and mix until you've removed all the lumps.

Pour the batter into the mug (do not fill more than halfway) and smooth the top with a spoon. Thump mug firmly on the tabletop six times to remove excess air bubbles. Place mug on top of a microwavable small plate or saucer.

Bake for 3 - 4 minutes. Check for doneness by inserting a toothpick in the middle of the microwave mug cake and removing the toothpick. If the toothpick is dry, the MMC is done.

Wait 2 minutes, then run a butter knife along the inside of the mug, and tip the cake into plate. Position the mug cake so that the slightly rounded top is on top. Your microwave mug cake will now look like a slightly overgrown muffin.

FANCY STUFF

Frost the whole Chocolate Chip Butterscotch Microwave Mug Cake with prepared butterscotch pudding chocolate frosting, or split the MMC in half, and frost each half individually (in which case you'll end up with two separate MMCs — or you can reassemble the frosted halves to create a layered MMC). Decorate, if you wish, with semi-sweet chocolate or butterscotch chips.

Chocolate Coconut Microwave Mug Cake

INGREDIENTS

1 egg
2 tablespoons sour cream
1 tablespoon oil
1/8 teaspoon vanilla extract
1/8 teaspoon baking powder
4 tablespoons sugar
2 tablespoons unsweetened
cocoa powder
4 tablespoons all-purpose flour
2 tablespoons shredded coconut

NOTE
Look, we're not asking you to shred the coconut. It comes already shredded in a bag. Sheesh.

DIRECTIONS

Prepare mug by coating the inside lightly with cooking spray.

Mix the ingredients in a small bowl. Beat egg first with a spoon and mix in other liquid ingredients. Then add dry ingredients and mix until you've removed all the lumps.

Pour the batter into the mug (do not fill more than halfway) and smooth the top with a spoon. Thump mug firmly on the tabletop six times to remove excess air bubbles. Place mug on top of a microwavable small plate or saucer.

Bake for 3 - 4 minutes. Check for doneness by inserting a toothpick in the middle of the microwave mug cake and removing the toothpick. If the toothpick is dry, the MMC is done.

Wait 2 minutes, then run a butter knife along the inside of the mug, and tip the cake into plate. Position the mug cake so that the slightly rounded top is on top. Your microwave mug cake will now look like a slightly overgrown muffin.

FANCY STUFF

Frost the whole Chocolate Coconut Microwave Mug Cake with chocolate frosting, or split the MMC in half, and frost each half individually (in which case you'll end up with two separate MMCs — or you can reassemble the frosted halves to create a layered MMC). Decorate, if you wish, with shredded coconut.

Chocolate Honey Raisin Microwave Mug Cake

INGREDIENTS
1 egg
2 tablespoons honey
2 tablespoons oil
1/8 teaspoon vanilla extract
1/8 teaspoon baking powder
1/4 teaspoon cinnamon
2 tablespoons sugar
4 tablespoons unsweetened
  cocoa powder
4 tablespoons all-purpose flour
2 tablespoons raisins

NOTE
As one of our intrepid MMC testers pointed out, there's no reason to limit your Chocolate Honey Raisin Microwave Mug Cake experience. Honey comes in all sorts of flavors. We encouraged him to try them all. And not to stray too far from a toilet.

DIRECTIONS
Prepare mug by coating the inside lightly with cooking spray.

Mix the ingredients in a small bowl. Beat egg first with a spoon and mix in other liquid ingredients. Then add dry ingredients and mix until you've removed all the lumps.

Pour the batter into the mug (do not fill more than halfway) and smooth the top with a spoon. Thump mug firmly on the tabletop six times to remove excess air bubbles. Place mug on top of a microwavable small plate or saucer.

Bake for 3 - 4 minutes. Check for doneness by inserting a toothpick in the middle of the microwave mug cake and removing the toothpick. If the toothpick is dry, the MMC is done.

Wait 2 minutes, then run a butter knife along the inside of the mug, and tip the cake into plate. Position the mug cake so that the slightly rounded top is on top. Your microwave mug cake will now look like a slightly overgrown muffin.

FANCY STUFF
Frost the whole Chocolate Honey Raisin Microwave Mug Cake with chocolate frosting, or split the MMC in half, and frost each half individually (in which case you'll end up with two separate MMCs — or you can reassemble the frosted halves to create a layered MMC). Decorate, if you wish, with raisins.

Chocolate Peach Microwave Mug Cake

INGREDIENTS

1 egg
2 tablespoons peach yogurt
   (with the fruit stirred in)
1 tablespoon oil
1/8 teaspoon vanilla extract
1/8 teaspoon baking powder
4 tablespoons sugar
2 tablespoons unsweetened
   cocoa powder
4 tablespoons all-purpose flour

NOTE
Some people have said that life is a bowl of peaches ... with the pits. Wait. No one has ever said that before.

DIRECTIONS

Prepare mug by coating the inside lightly with cooking spray.

Mix the ingredients in a small bowl. Beat egg first with a spoon and mix in other liquid ingredients. Then add dry ingredients and mix until you've removed all the lumps.

Pour the batter into the mug (do not fill more than halfway) and smooth the top with a spoon. Thump mug firmly on the tabletop six times to remove excess air bubbles. Place mug on top of a microwavable small plate or saucer.

Bake for 3 - 4 minutes. Check for doneness by inserting a toothpick in the middle of the microwave mug cake and removing the toothpick. If the toothpick is dry, the MMC is done.

Wait 2 minutes, then run a butter knife along the inside of the mug, and tip the cake into plate. Position the mug cake so that the slightly rounded top is on top. Your microwave mug cake will now look like a slightly overgrown muffin.

FANCY STUFF

Frost the whole Chocolate Peach Microwave Mug Cake with peach yogurt or chocolate frosting, or split the MMC in half, and frost each half individually (in which case you'll end up with two separate MMCs — or you can reassemble the frosted halves to create a layered MMC). Decorate, if you wish, with fresh or canned sliced peaches.

Chocolate Pistachio Microwave Mug Cake

INGREDIENTS

1 egg
3 tablespoons milk
3 tablespoons oil
1/8 teaspoon vanilla extract
1/8 teaspoon baking powder
4 tablespoons sugar
1 tablespoon instant pistachio
  pudding powder (not prepared)
1 tablespoon unsweetened
  cocoa powder
4 tablespoons all-purpose flour
2 tablespoons chopped pistachio nuts
  (optional)

NOTE
It isn't any easier for pistachio pudding to be green than it is for frogs.

DIRECTIONS

Prepare mug by coating the inside lightly with cooking spray.

Mix the ingredients in a small bowl. Beat egg first with a spoon and mix in other liquid ingredients. Then add dry ingredients and mix until you've removed all the lumps.

Pour the batter into the mug (do not fill more than halfway) and smooth the top with a spoon. Thump mug firmly on the tabletop six times to remove excess air bubbles. Place mug on top of a microwavable small plate or saucer.

Bake for 3 - 4 minutes. Check for doneness by inserting a toothpick in the middle of the microwave mug cake and removing the toothpick. If the toothpick is dry, the MMC is done.

Wait 2 minutes, then run a butter knife along the inside of the mug, and tip the cake into plate. Position the mug cake so that the slightly rounded top is on top. Your microwave mug cake will now look like a slightly overgrown muffin.

FANCY STUFF

Frost the whole Chocolate Pistachio Microwave Mug Cake with prepared pistachio pudding or chocolate frosting, or split the MMC in half, and frost each half individually (in which case you'll end up with two separate MMCs — or you can reassemble the frosted halves to create a layered MMC). Decorate, if you wish, with pistachio nuts.

Chocolate-Covered Cherry Microwave Mug Cake

INGREDIENTS

1 egg
1 tablespoon chocolate
   pudding (prepared)
2 tablespoons oil
1/8 teaspoon vanilla extract
1/8 teaspoon baking powder
4 tablespoons sugar
2 tablespoons instant cherry
   pudding powder (not prepared)
4 tablespoons all-purpose flour

NOTE
Do regular cherries ever feel sort of naked around chocolate-covered cherries?

DIRECTIONS

Prepare mug by coating the inside lightly with cooking spray.

Mix the ingredients in a small bowl. Beat egg first with a spoon and mix in other liquid ingredients. Then add dry ingredients and mix until you've removed all the lumps.

Pour the batter into the mug (do not fill more than halfway) and smooth the top with a spoon. Thump mug firmly on the tabletop six times to remove excess air bubbles. Place mug on top of a microwavable small plate or saucer.

Bake for 3 - 4 minutes. Check for doneness by inserting a toothpick in the middle of the microwave mug cake and removing the toothpick. If the toothpick is dry, the MMC is done.

Wait 2 minutes, then run a butter knife along the inside of the mug, and tip the cake into plate. Position the mug cake so that the slightly rounded top is on top. Your microwave mug cake will now look like a slightly overgrown muffin.

FANCY STUFF

Frost the whole Chocolate-Covered Cherry Microwave Mug Cake with chocolate pudding or chocolate frosting, or split the MMC in half, and frost each half individually (in which case you'll end up with two separate MMCs — or you can reassemble the frosted halves to create a layered MMC). Decorate, if you wish, with cherries.

Chocolate-Covered Peanut Microwave Mug Cake

INGREDIENTS

1 egg
1 tablespoon peanut butter
(smooth or chunky)
2 tablespoons milk
2 tablespoons oil
1/8 teaspoon vanilla extract
1/8 teaspoon of baking powder
4 tablespoons sugar
2 tablespoons unsweetened
cocoa powder
4 tablespoons all-purpose flour

NOTE
The Chocolate-Covered Peanut Microwave Mug Cake is named after a beloved cat we know named Peanut. We don't know any felines named Chocolate.

DIRECTIONS

Prepare mug by coating the inside lightly with cooking spray.

Mix the ingredients in a small bowl. Beat egg first with a spoon and mix in other liquid ingredients. Then add dry ingredients and mix until you've removed all the lumps.

Pour the batter into the mug (do not fill more than halfway) and smooth the top with a spoon. Thump mug firmly on the tabletop six times to remove excess air bubbles. Place mug on top of a microwavable small plate or saucer.

Bake for 3 - 4 minutes. Check for doneness by inserting a toothpick in the middle of the microwave mug cake and removing the toothpick. If the toothpick is dry, the MMC is done.

Wait 2 minutes, then run a butter knife along the inside of the mug, and tip the cake into plate. Position the mug cake so that the slightly rounded top is on top. Your microwave mug cake will now look like a slightly overgrown muffin.

FANCY STUFF

Frost the whole Chocolate-Covered Peanut Microwave Mug Cake with chocolate frosting or peanut butter, or split the MMC in half, and frost each half individually (in which case you'll end up with two separate MMCs — or you can reassemble the frosted halves to create a layered MMC). Decorate, if you wish, with peanuts.

Chocolate-Dipped Strawberry Microwave Mug Cake

INGREDIENTS

1 egg
2 tablespoons strawberry yogurt
  (with the fruit stirred in)
1 tablespoon oil
1/8 teaspoon of vanilla extract
1/8 teaspoon of baking powder
4 tablespoons sugar
2 tablespoons unsweetened
  cocoa powder
4 tablespoons all-purpose flour

NOTE
Someone might treat you to scrumptious chocolate-dipped strawberries on Valentine's Day, but don't count on it. This MMC's the backup plan.

DIRECTIONS

Prepare mug by coating the inside lightly with cooking spray.

Mix the ingredients in a small bowl. Beat egg first with a spoon and mix in other liquid ingredients. Then add dry ingredients and mix until you've removed all the lumps.

Pour the batter into the mug (do not fill more than halfway) and smooth the top with a spoon. Thump mug firmly on the tabletop six times to remove excess air bubbles. Place mug on top of a microwavable small plate or saucer.

Bake for 3 - 4 minutes. Check for doneness by inserting a toothpick in the middle of the microwave mug cake and removing the toothpick. If the toothpick is dry, the MMC is done.

Wait 2 minutes, then run a butter knife along the inside of the mug, and tip the cake into plate. Position the mug cake so that the slightly rounded top is on top. Your microwave mug cake will now look like a slightly overgrown muffin.

FANCY STUFF

Frost the whole Chocolate-Dipped Strawberry Microwave Mug Cake with strawberry yogurt or chocolate frosting, or split the MMC in half, and frost each half individually (in which case you'll end up with two separate MMCs — or you can reassemble the frosted halves to create a layered MMC). Decorate, if you wish, with fresh or frozen strawberries.

Chocolaty Banana Microwave Mug Cake

INGREDIENTS

1 egg
1 tablespoon banana baby food
1 tablespoon oil
1/8 teaspoon baking powder
1/8 teaspoon banana extract
  (or vanilla extract)
4 tablespoons sugar
2 tablespoons unsweetened
  cocoa powder
4 tablespoons all-purpose flour

NOTE
If you're looking at the word "chocolaty" and thinking — typo! — then we hate to disappoint you but "chocolaty" is the preferred spelling of the word, even though ""chocolatey" looks a whole lot better to us, too.

DIRECTIONS

Prepare mug by coating the inside lightly with cooking spray.

Mix the ingredients in a small bowl. Beat egg first with a spoon and mix in other liquid ingredients. Then add dry ingredients and mix until you've removed all the lumps.

Pour the batter into the mug (do not fill more than halfway) and smooth the top with a spoon. Thump mug firmly on the tabletop six times to remove excess air bubbles. Place mug on top of a microwavable small plate or saucer.

Bake for 3 - 4 minutes. Check for doneness by inserting a toothpick in the middle of the microwave mug cake and removing the toothpick. If the toothpick is dry, the MMC is done.

Wait 2 minutes, then run a butter knife along the inside of the mug, and tip the cake into plate. Position the mug cake so that the slightly rounded top is on top. Your microwave mug cake will now look like a slightly overgrown muffin.

FANCY STUFF

Frost the whole Chocolaty Banana Microwave Mug Cake with chocolate frosting, or split the MMC in half, and frost each half individually (in which case you'll end up with two separate MMCs — or you can reassemble the frosted halves to create a layered MMC). Decorate, if you wish, with sliced bananas (fresh or dried).

ChocoNana Chip Microwave Mug Cake

INGREDIENTS

1 egg
3 tablespoons milk
3 tablespoons oil
1/8 teaspoon vanilla extract
1/8 teaspoon baking powder
4 tablespoons sugar
1 tablespoon instant banana
 pudding powder (not prepared)
1 tablespoon unsweetened
 cocoa powder
4 tablespoons all-purpose flour
2 tablespoons white chocolate chips

NOTE

Are you one of those people who won't eat anything with a stupid name? Well, then, steer clear of the ChocoNana Chip Microwave Mug Cake. We'll bet you wouldn't mind singing a song about it, though.

DIRECTIONS

Prepare mug by coating the inside lightly with cooking spray.

Mix the ingredients in a small bowl. Beat egg first with a spoon and mix in other liquid ingredients. Then add dry ingredients and mix until you've removed all the lumps.

Pour the batter into the mug (do not fill more than halfway) and smooth the top with a spoon. Thump mug firmly on the tabletop six times to remove excess air bubbles. Place mug on top of a microwavable small plate or saucer.

Bake for 3 - 4 minutes. Check for doneness by inserting a toothpick in the middle of the microwave mug cake and removing the toothpick. If the toothpick is dry, the MMC is done.

Wait 2 minutes, then run a butter knife along the inside of the mug, and tip the cake into plate. Position the mug cake so that the slightly rounded top is on top. Your microwave mug cake will now look like a slightly overgrown muffin.

FANCY STUFF

Frost the whole ChocoNana Chip Microwave Mug Cake with prepared banana pudding or chocolate frosting, or split the MMC in half, and frost each half individually (in which case you'll end up with two separate MMCs — or you can reassemble the frosted halves to create a layered MMC). Decorate, if you wish, with white chocolate chips.

Chocopine Microwave Mug Cake

INGREDIENTS

1 egg
2 tablespoons pineapple yogurt
(with the fruit stirred in)
1 tablespoon oil
1/8 teaspoon vanilla extract
1/8 teaspoon baking powder
4 tablespoons sugar
2 tablespoons unsweetened
cocoa powder
4 tablespoons all-purpose flour

NOTE
Maybe the real problem is that anything starting with the prefix "Chocó" sounds foolish. Never, ever name anyone Chocó. Adding the suffix "pine" to the prefix "Chocó" won't help at all.

DIRECTIONS

Prepare mug by coating the inside lightly with cooking spray.

Mix the ingredients in a small bowl. Beat egg first with a spoon and mix in other liquid ingredients. Then add dry ingredients and mix until you've removed all the lumps.

Pour the batter into the mug (do not fill more than halfway) and smooth the top with a spoon. Thump mug firmly on the tabletop six times to remove excess air bubbles. Place mug on top of a microwavable small plate or saucer.

Bake for 3 - 4 minutes. Check for doneness by inserting a toothpick in the middle of the microwave mug cake and removing the toothpick. If the toothpick is dry, the MMC is done.

Wait 2 minutes, then run a butter knife along the inside of the mug, and tip the cake into plate. Position the mug cake so that the slightly rounded top is on top. Your microwave mug cake will now look like a slightly overgrown muffin.

FANCY STUFF

Frost the whole Chocopine Microwave Mug Cake with pineapple yogurt or your chocolate frosting, or split the MMC in half, and frost each half individually (in which case you'll end up with two separate MMCs — or you can reassemble the frosted halves to create a layered MMC). Decorate, if you wish, with pineapple chunks.

Cinnamon Pear Microwave Mug Cake

INGREDIENTS

1 egg
1 tablespoon pear baby food
1 tablespoon oil
1/8 teaspoon vanilla extract
1/8 teaspoon baking powder
1/4 teaspoon cinnamon
4 tablespoons light brown sugar
2 tablespoons instant vanilla
  pudding powder (not prepared)
4 tablespoons all-purpose flour

NOTE
If there's any such thing as a cinnamon pear, we want one!

DIRECTIONS

Prepare mug by coating the inside lightly with cooking spray.

Mix the ingredients in a small bowl. Beat egg first with a spoon and mix in other liquid ingredients. Then add dry ingredients and mix until you've removed all the lumps.

Pour the batter into the mug (do not fill more than halfway) and smooth the top with a spoon. Thump mug firmly on the tabletop six times to remove excess air bubbles. Place mug on top of a microwavable small plate or saucer.

Bake for 3 - 4 minutes. Check for doneness by inserting a toothpick in the middle of the microwave mug cake and removing the toothpick. If the toothpick is dry, the MMC is done.

Wait 2 minutes, then run a butter knife along the inside of the mug, and tip the cake into plate. Position the mug cake so that the slightly rounded top is on top. Your microwave mug cake will now look like a slightly overgrown muffin.

FANCY STUFF

Frost the whole Cinnamon Pear Microwave Mug Cake with prepared vanilla frosting, or split the MMC in half, and frost each half individually (in which case you'll end up with two separate MMCs — or you can reassemble the frosted halves to create a layered MMC). Decorate, if you wish, with sliced pears (fresh or canned).

Cocoblue Microwave Mug Cake

INGREDIENTS

1 egg
1 tablespoon blueberry pie filling
1 tablespoon oil
1/8 teaspoon vanilla extract
1/8 teaspoon baking powder
1/4 teaspoon cinnamon
4 tablespoons light brown sugar
2 tablespoons instant coconut
  cream pudding powder (not prepared)
4 tablespoons all-purpose flour
2 tablespoons dried blueberries

NOTE
At first blush, you'd think that the Cocoblue Microwave Mug Cake had cocoa in it, but you'd be wrong, because it has coconut in it instead. Nene.

DIRECTIONS

Prepare mug by coating the inside lightly with cooking spray.

Mix the ingredients in a small bowl. Beat egg first with a spoon and mix in other liquid ingredients. Then add dry ingredients and mix until you've removed all the lumps.

Pour the batter into the mug (do not fill more than halfway) and smooth the top with a spoon. Thump mug firmly on the tabletop six times to remove excess air bubbles. Place mug on top of a microwavable small plate or saucer.

Bake for 3 - 4 minutes. Check for doneness by inserting a toothpick in the middle of the microwave mug cake and removing the toothpick. If the toothpick is dry, the MMC is done.

Wait 2 minutes, then run a butter knife along the inside of the mug, and tip the cake into plate. Position the mug cake so that the slightly rounded top is on top. Your microwave mug cake will now look like a slightly overgrown muffin.

FANCY STUFF

Frost the whole Cocoblue Microwave Mug Cake with blueberry pie filling or the rest of the blueberry yogurt, or split the MMC in half, and frost each half individually (in which case you'll end up with two separate MMCs — or you can reassemble the frosted halves to create a layered MMC). Decorate, if you wish, with shredded coconut.

Coconut Butterscotch Chip Microwave Mug Cake

INGREDIENTS

1 egg
3 tablespoons milk
3 tablespoons oil
1/8 teaspoon vanilla extract
1/8 teaspoon baking powder
1/4 teaspoon cinnamon
4 tablespoons light brown sugar
2 tablespoons instant coconut
** cream pudding powder (not prepared)**
4 tablespoons all-purpose flour
2 tablespoons butterscotch chips

NOTE
Do you suppose that butterscotch chips are just wannabe chocolate chips who are trying to make a living until their big break comes along?

DIRECTIONS

Prepare mug by coating the inside lightly with cooking spray.

Mix the ingredients in a small bowl. Beat egg first with a spoon and mix in other liquid ingredients. Then add dry ingredients and mix until you've removed all the lumps.

Pour the batter into the mug (do not fill more than halfway) and smooth the top with a spoon. Thump mug firmly on the tabletop six times to remove excess air bubbles. Place mug on top of a microwavable small plate or saucer.

Bake for 3 - 4 minutes. Check for doneness by inserting a toothpick in the middle of the microwave mug cake and removing the toothpick. If the toothpick is dry, the MMC is done.

Wait 2 minutes, then run a butter knife along the inside of the mug, and tip the cake into plate. Position the mug cake so that the slightly rounded top is on top. Your microwave mug cake will now look like a slightly overgrown muffin.

FANCY STUFF

Frost the whole Coconut Butterscotch Chip Microwave Mug Cake with prepared butterscotch pudding, or split the MMC in half, and frost each half individually (in which case you'll end up with two separate MMCs — or you can reassemble the frosted halves to create a layered MMC). Decorate, if you wish, with shredded coconut.

Cranberry Chocolate Microwave Mug Cake

INGREDIENTS

1 egg
1 tablespoon jellied cranberry sauce
1 tablespoon oil
1/8 teaspoon vanilla extract
1/8 teaspoon baking powder
4 tablespoons sugar
2 tablespoons unsweetened
  cocoa powder
4 tablespoons all-purpose flour
2 tablespoons dried cranberries

NOTE
Here's the perfect MMC for people who hate turkey but love cranberry sauce and feel stupid just sitting there with their whole plate filled cranberry sauce.

DIRECTIONS

Prepare mug by coating the inside lightly with cooking spray.

Mix the ingredients in a small bowl. Beat egg first with a spoon and mix in other liquid ingredients. Then add dry ingredients and mix until you've removed all the lumps.

Pour the batter into the mug (do not fill more than halfway) and smooth the top with a spoon. Thump mug firmly on the tabletop six times to remove excess air bubbles. Place mug on top of a microwavable small plate or saucer.

Bake for 3 - 4 minutes. Check for doneness by inserting a toothpick in the middle of the microwave mug cake and removing the toothpick. If the toothpick is dry, the MMC is done.

Wait 2 minutes, then run a butter knife along the inside of the mug, and tip the cake into plate. Position the mug cake so that the slightly rounded top is on top. Your microwave mug cake will now look like a slightly overgrown muffin.

FANCY STUFF

Frost the whole Cranberry Chocolate Microwave Mug Cake with chocolate frosting, or split the MMC in half, and frost each half individually (in which case you'll end up with two separate MMCs — or you can reassemble the frosted halves to create a layered MMC). Decorate, if you wish, with dried cranberries.

Cranberry Lemon Microwave Mug Cake

INGREDIENTS

1 egg
1 tablespoon jellied
cranberry sauce
1 tablespoon oil
1/8 teaspoon vanilla extract
1/8 teaspoon baking powder
1/4 teaspoon cinnamon
4 tablespoons light brown sugar
2 tablespoons instant lemon
pudding powder (unprepared)
4 tablespoons all-purpose flour
2 tablespoons dried cranberries

NOTE
You'll almost want to see the
Cranberry Lemon Microwave Mug
Cake become a staple on your
Thanksgiving Day dinner table.

DIRECTIONS

Prepare mug by coating the inside lightly with cooking spray.

Mix the ingredients in a small bowl. Beat egg first with a spoon and mix
in other liquid ingredients. Then add dry ingredients and mix until you've
removed all the lumps.

Pour the batter into the mug (do not fill more than halfway) and smooth the
top with a spoon. Thump mug firmly on the tabletop six times to remove
excess air bubbles. Place mug on top of a microwavable small plate or saucer.

Bake for 3 - 4 minutes. Check for doneness by inserting a toothpick in the
middle of the microwave mug cake and removing the toothpick. If the
toothpick is dry, the MMC is done.

Wait 2 minutes, then run a butter knife along the inside of the mug, and tip
the cake into plate. Position the mug cake so that the slightly rounded top
is on top. Your microwave mug cake will now look like a slightly overgrown
muffin.

FANCY STUFF

Frost the whole Cranberry Lemon Microwave Mug Cake with lemon pie
filling or yogurt, or split the MMC in half, and frost each half individually (in
which case you'll end up with two separate MMCs — or you can reassemble
the frosted halves to create a layered MMC). Decorate, if you wish, with dried
cranberries.

Cranberry Yogurt Microwave Mug Cake

INGREDIENTS
1 egg
2 tablespoons Greek yogurt
1 tablespoon oil
1/8 teaspoon vanilla extract
1/8 teaspoon baking powder
1/4 teaspoon cinnamon
4 tablespoons sugar
2 tablespoons unsweetened
  cocoa powder
4 tablespoons all-purpose flour
2 tablespoons dried cranberries

NOTE
Greek yogurt may not taste like much when you eat it plain. But when you try some in an MMC, you'll be tempted to move to Greece!

DIRECTIONS
Prepare mug by coating the inside lightly with cooking spray.

Mix the ingredients in a small bowl. Beat egg first with a spoon and mix in other liquid ingredients. Then add dry ingredients and mix until you've removed all the lumps.

Pour the batter into the mug (do not fill more than halfway) and smooth the top with a spoon. Thump mug firmly on the tabletop six times to remove excess air bubbles. Place mug on top of a microwavable small plate or saucer.

Bake for 3 - 4 minutes. Check for doneness by inserting a toothpick in the middle of the microwave mug cake and removing the toothpick. If the toothpick is dry, the MMC is done.

Wait 2 minutes, then run a butter knife along the inside of the mug, and tip the cake into plate. Position the mug cake so that the slightly rounded top is on top. Your microwave mug cake will now look like a slightly overgrown muffin.

FANCY STUFF
Frost the whole Cranberry Yogurt Microwave Mug Cake with vanilla frosting, or split the MMC in half, and frost each half individually (in which case you'll end up with two separate MMCs — or you can reassemble the frosted halves to create a layered MMC). Decorate, if you wish, with dried cranberries.

Double Butterscotch Microwave Mug Cake

INGREDIENTS

1 egg
3 tablespoons milk
3 tablespoons oil
1/8 teaspoon vanilla extract
1/8 teaspoon baking powder
1/4 teaspoon cinnamon
4 tablespoons light brown sugar
2 tablespoons instant butterscotch
   pudding powder (not prepared)
4 tablespoons all-purpose flour
2 tablespoons butterscotch chips

NOTE
We flirted with the idea of calling the Double Butterscotch Microwave Mug Cake something like the Butter Butter Scotch Scotch Microwave Mug Cake, but then figured that sounded too stupid.

DIRECTIONS

Prepare mug by coating the inside lightly with cooking spray.

Mix the ingredients in a small bowl. Beat egg first with a spoon and mix in other liquid ingredients. Then add dry ingredients and mix until you've removed all the lumps.

Pour the batter into the mug (do not fill more than halfway) and smooth the top with a spoon. Thump mug firmly on the tabletop six times to remove excess air bubbles. Place mug on top of a microwavable small plate or saucer.

Bake for 3 - 4 minutes. Check for doneness by inserting a toothpick in the middle of the microwave mug cake and removing the toothpick. If the toothpick is dry, the MMC is done.

Wait 2 minutes, then run a butter knife along the inside of the mug, and tip the cake into plate. Position the mug cake so that the slightly rounded top is on top. Your microwave mug cake will now look like a slightly overgrown muffin.

FANCY STUFF

Frost the whole Double Butterscotch Microwave Mug Cake with prepared butterscotch pudding, or split the MMC in half, and frost each half individually (in which case you'll end up with two separate MMCs — or you can reassemble the frosted halves to create a layered MMC). Decorate, if you wish, with butterscotch chips.

Giant Grape Microwave Mug Cake

INGREDIENTS

1 egg
3 tablespoons unsweetened purple grape juice
2 tablespoons oil
1/8 teaspoon vanilla extract
1/8 teaspoon baking powder
4 tablespoons sugar
2 tablespoons grape instant gelatin powder (not prepared)
5 tablespoons all-purpose flour

NOTE
Remember that giant purple dinosaur who used to get beaten up a lot at shopping malls? Well, he had nothing to do with the Giant Grape Microwave Mug Cake, but he was something else, wasn't he?

DIRECTIONS

Prepare mug by coating the inside lightly with cooking spray.

Mix the ingredients in a small bowl. Beat egg first with a spoon and mix in other liquid ingredients. Then add dry ingredients and mix until you've removed all the lumps.

Pour the batter into the mug (do not fill more than halfway) and smooth the top with a spoon. Thump mug firmly on the tabletop six times to remove excess air bubbles. Place mug on top of a microwavable small plate or saucer.

Bake for 3 - 4 minutes. Check for doneness by inserting a toothpick in the middle of the microwave mug cake and removing the toothpick. If the toothpick is dry, the MMC is done.

Wait 2 minutes, then run a butter knife along the inside of the mug, and tip the cake into plate. Position the mug cake so that the slightly rounded top is on top. Your microwave mug cake will now look like a slightly overgrown muffin.

FANCY STUFF

Frost the whole Giant Grape Microwave Mug Cake with grape jelly, or split the MMC in half, and frost each half individually (in which case you'll end up with two separate MMCs — or you can reassemble the frosted halves to create a layered MMC). Decorate, if you wish, with powdered sugar.

Giant Orange Microwave Mug Cake

INGREDIENTS

1 egg
3 tablespoons orange juice
2 tablespoons oil
1/8 teaspoon vanilla extract
1/8 teaspoon baking powder
1/4 teaspoon cinnamon
4 tablespoons light brown sugar
2 tablespoons orange instant
  gelatin powder (not prepared)
5 tablespoons all-purpose flour

NOTE
Oranges are mostly about the same size, so if you ever see a giant one, it's probably the queen of oranges or something.

DIRECTIONS

Prepare mug by coating the inside lightly with cooking spray.

Mix the ingredients in a small bowl. Beat egg first with a spoon and mix in other liquid ingredients. Then add dry ingredients and mix until you've removed all the lumps.

Pour the batter into the mug (do not fill more than halfway) and smooth the top with a spoon. Thump mug firmly on the tabletop six times to remove excess air bubbles. Place mug on top of a microwavable small plate or saucer.

Bake for 3 - 4 minutes. Check for doneness by inserting a toothpick in the middle of the microwave mug cake and removing the toothpick. If the toothpick is dry, the MMC is done.

Wait 2 minutes, then run a butter knife along the inside of the mug, and tip the cake into plate. Position the mug cake so that the slightly rounded top is on top. Your microwave mug cake will now look like a slightly overgrown muffin.

FANCY STUFF

Frost the whole Giant Orange Microwave Mug Cake with orange marmalade, or split the MMC in half, and frost each half individually (in which case you'll end up with two separate MMCs — or you can reassemble the frosted halves to create a layered MMC). Decorate, if you wish, with slices of an orange.

Ginger Coconut Microwave Mug Cake

INGREDIENTS

1 egg
3 tablespoons milk
3 tablespoons oil
1/8 teaspoon vanilla extract
1/8 teaspoon baking powder
1/4 teaspoon ginger
4 tablespoons light brown sugar
2 tablespoons instant coconut
  pudding powder (not prepared)
4 tablespoons all-purpose flour
2 tablespoons shredded coconut

NOTE
Naturally, Ginger ate coconuts on that deserted island from the classic television show.
So maybe she was the inspiration for the Ginger Coconut Microwave Mug Cake. Or maybe not.

DIRECTIONS

Prepare mug by coating the inside lightly with cooking spray.

Mix the ingredients in a small bowl. Beat egg first with a spoon and mix in other liquid ingredients. Then add dry ingredients and mix until you've removed all the lumps.

Pour the batter into the mug (do not fill more than halfway) and smooth the top with a spoon. Thump mug firmly on the tabletop six times to remove excess air bubbles. Place mug on top of a microwavable small plate or saucer.

Bake for 3 - 4 minutes. Check for doneness by inserting a toothpick in the middle of the microwave mug cake and removing the toothpick. If the toothpick is dry, the MMC is done.

Wait 2 minutes, then run a butter knife along the inside of the mug, and tip the cake into plate. Position the mug cake so that the slightly rounded top is on top. Your microwave mug cake will now look like a slightly overgrown muffin.

FANCY STUFF

Frost the whole Ginger Coconut Microwave Mug Cake with coconut frosting, or split the MMC in half, and frost each half individually (in which case you'll end up with two separate MMCs — or you can reassemble the frosted halves to create a layered MMC). Decorate, if you wish, with shredded coconut.

Gingerberry Microwave Mug Cake

INGREDIENTS

1 egg
2 tablespoons mixed berry yogurt
   (with the fruit stirred in)
1 tablespoon oil
1/8 teaspoon vanilla extract
1/8 teaspoon baking powder
1/4 teaspoon ginger
4 tablespoons light brown sugar
2 tablespoons instant vanilla
   pudding powder (not prepared)
4 tablespoons all-purpose flour

NOTE
You don't find many berries named Ginger these days.

DIRECTIONS

Prepare mug by coating the inside lightly with cooking spray.

Mix the ingredients in a small bowl. Beat egg first with a spoon and mix in other liquid ingredients. Then add dry ingredients and mix until you've removed all the lumps.

Pour the batter into the mug (do not fill more than halfway) and smooth the top with a spoon. Thump mug firmly on the tabletop six times to remove excess air bubbles. Place mug on top of a microwavable small plate or saucer.

Bake for 3 - 4 minutes. Check for doneness by inserting a toothpick in the middle of the microwave mug cake and removing the toothpick. If the toothpick is dry, the MMC is done.

Wait 2 minutes, then run a butter knife along the inside of the mug, and tip the cake into plate. Position the mug cake so that the slightly rounded top is on top. Your microwave mug cake will now look like a slightly overgrown muffin.

FANCY STUFF

Frost the whole Gingerberry Microwave Mug Cake with mixed berry yogurt, or split the MMC in half, and frost each half individually (in which case you'll end up with two separate MMCs — or you can reassemble the frosted halves to create a layered MMC). Decorate, if you wish, fresh or frozen blueberries.

Grapilla Microwave Mug Cake

INGREDIENTS
1 egg
1 tablespoon vanilla pudding
(prepared)
2 tablespoons oil
1/8 teaspoon vanilla extract
1/8 teaspoon baking powder
1/4 teaspoon cinnamon
4 tablespoons light brown sugar
2 tablespoons grape instant
gelatin powder (not prepared)
4 tablespoons all-purpose flour

NOTE
In some parts of the world, the word "grapilla" is pronounced "gray - pee -ya." But don't let that stop you from enjoying the Grapilla Microwave Mug Cake.

DIRECTIONS
Prepare mug by coating the inside lightly with cooking spray.

Mix the ingredients in a small bowl. Beat egg first with a spoon and mix in other liquid ingredients. Then add dry ingredients and mix until you've removed all the lumps.

Pour the batter into the mug (do not fill more than halfway) and smooth the top with a spoon. Thump mug firmly on the tabletop six times to remove excess air bubbles. Place mug on top of a microwavable small plate or saucer.

Bake for 3 - 4 minutes. Check for doneness by inserting a toothpick in the middle of the microwave mug cake and removing the toothpick. If the toothpick is dry, the MMC is done.

Wait 2 minutes, then run a butter knife along the inside of the mug, and tip the cake into plate. Position the mug cake so that the slightly rounded top is on top. Your microwave mug cake will now look like a slightly overgrown muffin.

FANCY STUFF
Frost the whole Grapilla Microwave Mug Cake with vanilla pudding, vanilla frosting, or grape jelly, or split the MMC in half, and frost each half individually (in which case you'll end up with two separate MMCs — or you can reassemble the frosted halves to create a layered MMC). Decorate, if you wish, with powdered sugar.

Heavenly Chocolate Microwave Mug Cake

INGREDIENTS

1 egg
1 tablespoon chocolate pudding
  (prepared)
2 tablespoons oil
1/8 teaspoon vanilla extract
1/8 teaspoon baking powder
4 tablespoons sugar
2 tablespoons unsweetened
  cocoa powder
4 tablespoons all-purpose flour
2 tablespoons white chocolate chips

NOTE
Are heavenly desserts eligible for sainthood?

DIRECTIONS

Prepare mug by coating the inside lightly with cooking spray.

Mix the ingredients in a small bowl. Beat egg first with a spoon and mix in other liquid ingredients. Then add dry ingredients and mix until you've removed all the lumps.

Pour the batter into the mug (do not fill more than halfway) and smooth the top with a spoon. Thump mug firmly on the tabletop six times to remove excess air bubbles. Place mug on top of a microwavable small plate or saucer.

Bake for 3 - 4 minutes. Check for doneness by inserting a toothpick in the middle of the microwave mug cake and removing the toothpick. If the toothpick is dry, the MMC is done.

Wait 2 minutes, then run a butter knife along the inside of the mug, and tip the cake into plate. Position the mug cake so that the slightly rounded top is on top. Your microwave mug cake will now look like a slightly overgrown muffin.

FANCY STUFF

Frost the whole Heavenly Chocolate Microwave Mug Cake with chocolate pudding or chocolate frosting, or split the MMC in half, and frost each half individually (in which case you'll end up with two separate MMCs — or you can reassemble the frosted halves to create a layered MMC). Decorate, if you wish, with white chocolate chips.

Honey Coconut Microwave Mug Cake

INGREDIENTS

1 egg
2 tablespoons honey
2 tablespoons oil
1/8 teaspoon vanilla extract
1/8 teaspoon baking powder
1/4 teaspoon cinnamon
2 tablespoons light brown sugar
**4 tablespoons instant coconut
  cream pudding powder (not prepared)**
4 tablespoons all-purpose flour
2 tablespoons dried cranberries

NOTE
One of our intrepid MMC testers described the Honey Coconut Microwave Mug Cake as her favorite. Good pick!

DIRECTIONS

Prepare mug by coating the inside lightly with cooking spray.

Mix the ingredients in a small bowl. Beat egg first with a spoon and mix in other liquid ingredients. Then add dry ingredients and mix until you've removed all the lumps.

Pour the batter into the mug (do not fill more than halfway) and smooth the top with a spoon. Thump mug firmly on the tabletop six times to remove excess air bubbles. Place mug on top of a microwavable small plate or saucer.

Bake for 3 - 4 minutes. Check for doneness by inserting a toothpick in the middle of the microwave mug cake and removing the toothpick. If the toothpick is dry, the MMC is done.

Wait 2 minutes, then run a butter knife along the inside of the mug, and tip the cake into plate. Position the mug cake so that the slightly rounded top is on top. Your microwave mug cake will now look like a slightly overgrown muffin.

FANCY STUFF

Frost the whole Honey Coconut Microwave Mug Cake with coconut frosting, or split the MMC in half, and frost each half individually (in which case you'll end up with two separate MMCs — or you can reassemble the frosted halves to create a layered MMC). Decorate, if you wish, with dried cranberries or shredded coconut.

Honey Walnut Microwave Mug Cake

INGREDIENTS
1 egg
2 tablespoons honey
2 tablespoons oil
1/8 teaspoon vanilla extract
1/8 teaspoon baking powder
1/4 teaspoon cinnamon
2 tablespoons light brown sugar
**4 tablespoons instant vanilla
   pudding powder (not prepared)**
4 tablespoons all-purpose flour
2 tablespoons chopped walnuts

NOTE
*Why don't they ever talk about the
Land of Walnuts and Honey? It
just seems like an oversight. That's
all we're saying.*

DIRECTIONS
Prepare mug by coating the inside lightly with cooking spray.

Mix the ingredients in a small bowl. Beat egg first with a spoon and mix
in other liquid ingredients. Then add dry ingredients and mix until you've
removed all the lumps.

Pour the batter into the mug (do not fill more than halfway) and smooth the
top with a spoon. Thump mug firmly on the tabletop six times to remove
excess air bubbles. Place mug on top of a microwavable small plate or saucer.

Bake for 3 - 4 minutes. Check for doneness by inserting a toothpick in the
middle of the microwave mug cake and removing the toothpick. If the
toothpick is dry, the MMC is done.

Wait 2 minutes, then run a butter knife along the inside of the mug, and tip
the cake into plate. Position the mug cake so that the slightly rounded top
is on top. Your microwave mug cake will now look like a slightly overgrown
muffin.

FANCY STUFF
Frost the whole Honey Walnut Microwave Mug Cake with vanilla frosting, or
split the MMC in half, and frost each half individually (in which case you'll end
up with two separate MMCs — or you can reassemble the frosted halves to
create a layered MMC). Decorate, if you wish, with chopped walnuts.

Lemon and Lime Microwave Mug Cake

INGREDIENTS
1 egg
2 tablespoons lemon yogurt
1 tablespoon oil
1/8 teaspoon vanilla extract
1/8 teaspoon baking powder
1/4 teaspoon cinnamon
4 tablespoons light brown sugar
2 tablespoons lime instant gelatin
  powder (not prepared)
4 tablespoons all-purpose flour

NOTE
Do you have a hard time making decisions? Well, this might make your life a little bit easier. Now you won't have to choose between lemon and lime. Yes! You can have both of them!

DIRECTIONS
Prepare mug by coating the inside lightly with cooking spray.

Mix the ingredients in a small bowl. Beat egg first with a spoon and mix in other liquid ingredients. Then add dry ingredients and mix until you've removed all the lumps.

Pour the batter into the mug (do not fill more than halfway) and smooth the top with a spoon. Thump mug firmly on the tabletop six times to remove excess air bubbles. Place mug on top of a microwavable small plate or saucer.

Bake for 3 - 4 minutes. Check for doneness by inserting a toothpick in the middle of the microwave mug cake and removing the toothpick. If the toothpick is dry, the MMC is done.

Wait 2 minutes, then run a butter knife along the inside of the mug, and tip the cake into plate. Position the mug cake so that the slightly rounded top is on top. Your microwave mug cake will now look like a slightly overgrown muffin.

FANCY STUFF
Frost the whole Lemon and Lime Microwave Mug Cake with lemon yogurt or lemon pie filling, or split the MMC in half, and frost each half individually (in which case you'll end up with two separate MMCs — or you can reassemble the frosted halves to create a layered MMC). Decorate, if you wish, with powdered sugar.

Lemon Cherry Microwave Mug Cake

INGREDIENTS

1 egg
2 tablespoons lemon yogurt
1 tablespoon oil
1/8 teaspoon vanilla extract
1/8 teaspoon baking powder
1/4 teaspoon cinnamon
4 tablespoons light brown sugar
2 tablespoons instant cherry
  gelatin powder (not prepared)
4 tablespoons all-purpose flour

NOTE
If life hands you cherries, why can't you make cherronade?

DIRECTIONS

Prepare mug by coating the inside lightly with cooking spray.

Mix the ingredients in a small bowl. Beat egg first with a spoon and mix in other liquid ingredients. Then add dry ingredients and mix until you've removed all the lumps.

Pour the batter into the mug (do not fill more than halfway) and smooth the top with a spoon. Thump mug firmly on the tabletop six times to remove excess air bubbles. Place mug on top of a microwavable small plate or saucer.

Bake for 3 - 4 minutes. Check for doneness by inserting a toothpick in the middle of the microwave mug cake and removing the toothpick. If the toothpick is dry, the MMC is done.

Wait 2 minutes, then run a butter knife along the inside of the mug, and tip the cake into plate. Position the mug cake so that the slightly rounded top is on top. Your microwave mug cake will now look like a slightly overgrown muffin.

FANCY STUFF

Frost the whole Lemon Cherry Microwave Mug Cake with lemon yogurt or lemon pie filling, or split the MMC in half, and frost each half individually (in which case you'll end up with two separate MMCs — or you can reassemble the frosted halves to create a layered MMC). Decorate, if you wish, with cherries.

Lemon Ginger Microwave Mug Cake

INGREDIENTS

1 egg
3 tablespoons lemonade (prepared)
1 tablespoon oil
1/8 teaspoon lemon extract
  (or vanilla extract)
1/8 teaspoon baking powder
1/4 teaspoon ginger
4 tablespoons light brown sugar
2 tablespoons instant lemon
  pudding powder (not prepared)
5 tablespoons all-purpose flour

NOTE
When life hands you lemons, you can make the Lemon Ginger Microwave Mug Cake. Then again, life would also have to hand you ginger at the same time, and what are the chances of that happening?

DIRECTIONS

Prepare mug by coating the inside lightly with cooking spray.

Mix the ingredients in a small bowl. Beat egg first with a spoon and mix in other liquid ingredients. Then add dry ingredients and mix until you've removed all the lumps.

Pour the batter into the mug (do not fill more than halfway) and smooth the top with a spoon. Thump mug firmly on the tabletop six times to remove excess air bubbles. Place mug on top of a microwavable small plate or saucer.

Bake for 3 - 4 minutes. Check for doneness by inserting a toothpick in the middle of the microwave mug cake and removing the toothpick. If the toothpick is dry, the MMC is done.

Wait 2 minutes, then run a butter knife along the inside of the mug, and tip the cake into plate. Position the mug cake so that the slightly rounded top is on top. Your microwave mug cake will now look like a slightly overgrown muffin.

FANCY STUFF

Frost the whole Lemon Ginger Microwave Mug Cake with lemon yogurt or lemon pie filling, or split the MMC in half, and frost each half individually (in which case you'll end up with two separate MMCs — or you can reassemble the frosted halves to create a layered MMC). Decorate, if you wish, with small candies, or with candied ginger.

Lemon Poppy Seed Microwave Mug Cake

INGREDIENTS

1 egg
2 tablespoons lemon yogurt
1 tablespoon oil
1/8 teaspoon vanilla extract
1/8 teaspoon baking powder
1/4 teaspoon cinnamon
4 tablespoons light brown sugar
2 tablespoons instant lemon
  pudding powder (not prepared)
4 tablespoons all-purpose flour
1 tablespoon poppy seeds

NOTE
Lemon and poppy seed desserts seem pretty chic until you get some poppy seeds stuck in your front teeth.

DIRECTIONS

Prepare mug by coating the inside lightly with cooking spray.

Mix the ingredients in a small bowl. Beat egg first with a spoon and mix in other liquid ingredients. Then add dry ingredients and mix until you've removed all the lumps.

Pour the batter into the mug (do not fill more than halfway) and smooth the top with a spoon. Thump mug firmly on the tabletop six times to remove excess air bubbles. Place mug on top of a microwavable small plate or saucer.

Bake for 3 - 4 minutes. Check for doneness by inserting a toothpick in the middle of the microwave mug cake and removing the toothpick. If the toothpick is dry, the MMC is done.

Wait 2 minutes, then run a butter knife along the inside of the mug, and tip the cake into plate. Position the mug cake so that the slightly rounded top is on top. Your microwave mug cake will now look like a slightly overgrown muffin.

FANCY STUFF

Frost the whole Lemon Poppy Seed Microwave Mug Cake with lemon yogurt or lemon pie filling, or split the MMC in half, and frost each half individually (in which case you'll end up with two separate MMCs — or you can reassemble the frosted halves to create a layered MMC). Decorate, if you wish, with fruit, or sprinkle with poppy seeds.

Lemon Pound Microwave Mug Cake

INGREDIENTS

1 egg
2 tablespoons sour cream
1 tablespoon butter
(room temperature)
1/8 teaspoon vanilla extract
1/8 teaspoon baking powder
1/4 teaspoon cinnamon
4 tablespoons light brown sugar
2 tablespoons instant lemon
pudding powder (not prepared)
4 tablespoons all-purpose flour
1/4 teaspoon lemon zest (optional)

NOTE
Legend has it that the pound cake gets its name because the original used a pound, each, of sugar, flour, and eggs. That said, we have no idea where the Lemon Pound Microwave Mug Cake gets its name. We might have to invent a legend.

DIRECTIONS

Prepare mug by coating the inside lightly with cooking spray.

Mix the ingredients in a small bowl. Beat egg first with a spoon and mix in other liquid ingredients. Then add dry ingredients and mix until you've removed all the lumps.

Pour the batter into the mug (do not fill more than halfway) and smooth the top with a spoon. Thump mug firmly on the tabletop six times to remove excess air bubbles. Place mug on top of a microwavable small plate or saucer.

Bake for 3 - 4 minutes. Check for doneness by inserting a toothpick in the middle of the microwave mug cake and removing the toothpick. If the toothpick is dry, the MMC is done.

Wait 2 minutes, then run a butter knife along the inside of the mug, and tip the cake into plate. Position the mug cake so that the slightly rounded top is on top. Your microwave mug cake will now look like a slightly overgrown muffin.

FANCY STUFF

Frost the whole Lemon Pound Microwave Mug Cake with lemon yogurt or lemon pie filling, or split the MMC in half, and frost each half individually (in which case you'll end up with two separate MMCs — or you can reassemble the frosted halves to create a layered MMC). Decorate, if you wish, with small candies such as gumdrops.

Lemon Raspberry Microwave Mug Cake

INGREDIENTS

1 egg
2 tablespoons lemon yogurt
1 tablespoon oil
1/8 teaspoon vanilla extract
1/8 teaspoon baking powder
1/4 teaspoon cinnamon
4 tablespoons light brown sugar
2 tablespoons raspberry instant
  gelatin powder (not prepared)
4 tablespoons all-purpose flour

NOTE
A raspberry is the rude sound a lemon would make if a lemon used its tongue to blow air out of its mouth — presuming a lemon had either a tongue or a mouth.

DIRECTIONS

Prepare mug by coating the inside lightly with cooking spray.

Mix the ingredients in a small bowl. Beat egg first with a spoon and mix in other liquid ingredients. Then add dry ingredients and mix until you've removed all the lumps.

Pour the batter into the mug (do not fill more than halfway) and smooth the top with a spoon. Thump mug firmly on the tabletop six times to remove excess air bubbles. Place mug on top of a microwavable small plate or saucer.

Bake for 3 - 4 minutes. Check for doneness by inserting a toothpick in the middle of the microwave mug cake and removing the toothpick. If the toothpick is dry, the MMC is done.

Wait 2 minutes, then run a butter knife along the inside of the mug, and tip the cake into plate. Position the mug cake so that the slightly rounded top is on top. Your microwave mug cake will now look like a slightly overgrown muffin.

FANCY STUFF

Frost the whole Lemon Raspberry Microwave Mug Cake with lemon yogurt or raspberry jelly, or split the MMC in half, and frost each half individually (in which case you'll end up with two separate MMCs — or you can reassemble the frosted halves to create a layered MMC). Decorate, if you wish, with fresh or frozen raspberries.

Lemonberry Microwave Mug Cake

INGREDIENTS
1 egg
1 tablespoon strawberry
  sundae syrup
1 tablespoon oil
1/8 teaspoon vanilla extract
1/8 teaspoon baking powder
1/4 teaspoon cinnamon
4 tablespoons light brown sugar
2 tablespoons instant lemon
  pudding powder (not prepared)
4 tablespoons all-purpose flour

NOTE
*Why don't they call it a hot
strawberry sundae if the sundae
is made with strawberry sundae
syrup instead of hot fudge syrup?*

DIRECTIONS
Prepare mug by coating the inside lightly with cooking spray.

Mix the ingredients in a small bowl. Beat egg first with a spoon and mix
in other liquid ingredients. Then add dry ingredients and mix until you've
removed all the lumps.

Pour the batter into the mug (do not fill more than halfway) and smooth the
top with a spoon. Thump mug firmly on the tabletop six times to remove
excess air bubbles. Place mug on top of a microwavable small plate or saucer.

Bake for 3 - 4 minutes. Check for doneness by inserting a toothpick in the
middle of the microwave mug cake and removing the toothpick. If the
toothpick is dry, the MMC is done.

Wait 2 minutes, then run a butter knife along the inside of the mug, and tip
the cake into plate. Position the mug cake so that the slightly rounded top
is on top. Your microwave mug cake will now look like a slightly overgrown
muffin.

FANCY STUFF
Frost the whole Lemonberry Microwave Mug Cake with lemon yogurt or
lemon pie filling, or split the MMC in half, and frost each half individually (in
which case you'll end up with two separate MMCs — or you can reassemble
the frosted halves to create a layered MMC). Decorate, if you wish, with fresh
or frozen strawberries or strawberry syrup.

Lemonscotch Microwave Mug Cake

INGREDIENTS
1 egg
1 tablespoon lemon pie filling
1 tablespoon oil
1/8 teaspoon vanilla extract
1/8 teaspoon baking powder
1/4 teaspoon cinnamon
4 tablespoons light brown sugar
2 tablespoons instant butterscotch
pudding powder (not prepared)
4 tablespoons all-purpose flour

NOTE
Have you ever tried to play hopscotch while eating a Lemonscotch Microwave Mug Cake? That could be pretty interesting!

DIRECTIONS
Prepare mug by coating the inside lightly with cooking spray.

Mix the ingredients in a small bowl. Beat egg first with a spoon and mix in other liquid ingredients. Then add dry ingredients and mix until you've removed all the lumps.

Pour the batter into the mug (do not fill more than halfway) and smooth the top with a spoon. Thump mug firmly on the tabletop six times to remove excess air bubbles. Place mug on top of a microwavable small plate or saucer.

Bake for 3 - 4 minutes. Check for doneness by inserting a toothpick in the middle of the microwave mug cake and removing the toothpick. If the toothpick is dry, the MMC is done.

Wait 2 minutes, then run a butter knife along the inside of the mug, and tip the cake into plate. Position the mug cake so that the slightly rounded top is on top. Your microwave mug cake will now look like a slightly overgrown muffin.

FANCY STUFF
Frost the whole Lemonscotch Microwave Mug Cake with lemon yogurt or lemon pie filling, or split the MMC in half, and frost each half individually (in which case you'll end up with two separate MMCs — or you can reassemble the frosted halves to create a layered MMC). Decorate, if you wish, with butterscotch chips.

Lemorange Microwave Mug Cake

INGREDIENTS

1 egg
2 tablespoons lemon yogurt
1 tablespoon oil
1/8 teaspoon vanilla extract
1/8 teaspoon baking powder
1/4 teaspoon cinnamon
4 tablespoons light brown sugar
2 tablespoons orange instant
   gelatin powder (not prepared)
4 tablespoons all-purpose flour

NOTE
Some people are lucky enough to live in places where they can pick fresh lemons and oranges from trees every morning. Others of us have to pick our fruit out of yogurt containers and packages of gelatin powder.

DIRECTIONS

Prepare mug by coating the inside lightly with cooking spray.

Mix the ingredients in a small bowl. Beat egg first with a spoon and mix in other liquid ingredients. Then add dry ingredients and mix until you've removed all the lumps.

Pour the batter into the mug (do not fill more than halfway) and smooth the top with a spoon. Thump mug firmly on the tabletop six times to remove excess air bubbles. Place mug on top of a microwavable small plate or saucer.

Bake for 3 - 4 minutes. Check for doneness by inserting a toothpick in the middle of the microwave mug cake and removing the toothpick. If the toothpick is dry, the MMC is done.

Wait 2 minutes, then run a butter knife along the inside of the mug, and tip the cake into plate. Position the mug cake so that the slightly rounded top is on top. Your microwave mug cake will now look like a slightly overgrown muffin.

FANCY STUFF

Frost the whole Lemorange Microwave Mug Cake with prepared lemon yogurt or lemon pie filling, or split the MMC in half, and frost each half individually (in which case you'll end up with two separate MMCs — or you can reassemble the frosted halves to create a layered MMC). Decorate, if you wish, with small candies such as gumdrops.

Lime Green Tea Microwave Mug Cake

INGREDIENTS

1 egg

2 tablespoon oil

3 tablespoons green tea
  (Refer To Note on Right)

1/8 teaspoon vanilla extract

1/8 teaspoon baking powder

4 tablespoons light brown sugar

2 tablespoons lime instant gelatin
  powder (not prepared)

5 tablespoons all-purpose flour

HOW TO...
Boil five tablespoons of water, and then steep a green tea teabag in it for five minutes. Remove the teabag, and measure three tablespoons of tea into batter. Discard any remaining tea.

NOTE
It seems as though green tea is everywhere these days: in soap, juice, shampoo, bacon, windshield wiper fluid, gasoline, and more. So why shouldn't it also be in an MMC?

DIRECTIONS

Prepare mug by coating the inside lightly with cooking spray.

Mix the ingredients in a small bowl. Beat egg first with a spoon and mix in other liquid ingredients. Then add dry ingredients and mix until you've removed all the lumps.

Pour the batter into the mug (do not fill more than halfway) and smooth the top with a spoon. Thump mug firmly on the tabletop six times to remove excess air bubbles. Place mug on top of a microwavable small plate or saucer.

Bake for 3 - 4 minutes. Check for doneness by inserting a toothpick in the middle of the microwave mug cake and removing the toothpick. If the toothpick is dry, the MMC is done.

Wait 2 minutes, then run a butter knife along the inside of the mug, and tip the cake into plate. Position the mug cake so that the slightly rounded top is on top. Your microwave mug cake will now look like a slightly overgrown muffin.

FANCY STUFF

Frost the whole Lime Green Tea Microwave Mug Cake with vanilla frosting, or split the MMC in half, and frost each half individually (in which case you'll end up with two separate MMCs — or you can reassemble the frosted halves to create a layered MMC). Decorate, if you wish, with small candies such as gumdrops.

Maple Walnut Microwave Mug Cake

INGREDIENTS

1 egg
3 tablespoons maple syrup
3 tablespoons oil
1/8 teaspoon maple extract
  (or vanilla extract)
1/8 teaspoon baking powder
2 tablespoons light brown sugar
2 tablespoons instant vanilla
  pudding powder (not prepared)
4 tablespoons all-purpose flour
2 tablespoons chopped walnuts

NOTE

Do not use pure maple syrup to make a Maple Walnut Microwave Mug Cake. In the first place, that stuff's expensive. In the second place (with apologies to our friends who live in Canada and Vermont), the cheap watery stuff works better for this recipe. Our team of intrepid MMC testers report that they used a store brand that contains 5 percent real maple syrup to make their samples, and it worked out perfectly.

DIRECTIONS

Prepare mug by coating the inside lightly with cooking spray.

Mix the ingredients in a small bowl. Beat egg first with a spoon and mix in other liquid ingredients. Then add dry ingredients and mix until you've removed all the lumps.

Pour the batter into the mug (do not fill more than halfway) and smooth the top with a spoon. Thump mug firmly on the tabletop six times to remove excess air bubbles. Place mug on top of a microwavable small plate or saucer.

Bake for 3 - 4 minutes. Check for doneness by inserting a toothpick in the middle of the microwave mug cake and removing the toothpick. If the toothpick is dry, the MMC is done.

Wait 2 minutes, then run a butter knife along the inside of the mug, and tip the cake into plate. Position the mug cake so that the slightly rounded top is on top. Your microwave mug cake will now look like a slightly overgrown muffin.

FANCY STUFF

Frost the whole Maple Walnut Microwave Mug Cake with maple syrup. Decorate, if you wish, with chopped walnuts.

Mm(mm) Microwave Mug Cake

INGREDIENTS

1 egg
3 tablespoons milk
3 tablespoon oil
1/8 teaspoon baking powder
1/8 teaspoon vanilla extract
4 tablespoons sugar
2 tablespoons unsweetened
  cocoa powder
4 tablespoons all-purpose flour
2 tablespoons M&M'S® Minis®

NOTE
How great is it that we now have blue M&M'S® in our lives? We hardly even miss the light brown ones anymore.

DIRECTIONS

Prepare mug by coating the inside lightly with cooking spray.

Mix the ingredients in a small bowl. Beat egg first with a spoon and mix in other liquid ingredients. Then add dry ingredients and mix until you've removed all the lumps.

Pour the batter into the mug (do not fill more than halfway) and smooth the top with a spoon. Thump mug firmly on the tabletop six times to remove excess air bubbles. Place mug on top of a microwavable small plate or saucer.

Bake for 3 - 4 minutes. Check for doneness by inserting a toothpick in the middle of the microwave mug cake and removing the toothpick. If the toothpick is dry, the MMC is done.

Wait 2 minutes, then run a butter knife along the inside of the mug, and tip the cake into plate. Position the mug cake so that the slightly rounded top is on top. Your microwave mug cake will now look like a slightly overgrown muffin.

FANCY STUFF

Frost the whole Mm(mm) Microwave Mug Cake with chocolate frosting, or split the MMC in half, and frost each half individually (in which case you'll end up with two separate MMCs — or you can reassemble the frosted halves to create a layered MMC). Decorate, if you wish, with M&M'S® Minis®.

Mocha Microwave Mug Cake

INGREDIENTS

1 egg
1 tablespoon chocolate pudding
  (prepared)
2 tablespoons oil
1/8 teaspoon vanilla extract
1/8 teaspoon of baking powder
1/4 teaspoon instant coffee
  (unprepared)
4 tablespoons sugar
2 tablespoons unsweetened
  cocoa powder
4 tablespoons all-purpose flour

NOTE
*Single-serving coffee makers
are fine, but those lovely orange
envelopes with freeze-dried
instant coffee granules inside are
a lot cheaper. Try one.*

DIRECTIONS

Prepare mug by coating the inside lightly with cooking spray.

Mix the ingredients in a small bowl. Beat egg first with a spoon and mix
in other liquid ingredients. Then add dry ingredients and mix until you've
removed all the lumps.

Pour the batter into the mug (do not fill more than halfway) and smooth the
top with a spoon. Thump mug firmly on the tabletop six times to remove
excess air bubbles. Place mug on top of a microwavable small plate or saucer.

Bake for 3 - 4 minutes. Check for doneness by inserting a toothpick in the
middle of the microwave mug cake and removing the toothpick. If the
toothpick is dry, the MMC is done.

Wait 2 minutes, then run a butter knife along the inside of the mug, and tip
the cake into plate. Position the mug cake so that the slightly rounded top
is on top. Your microwave mug cake will now look like a slightly overgrown
muffin.

FANCY STUFF

Frost the whole Mocha Microwave Mug Cake with chocolate or mocha
frosting, or split the MMC in half, and frost each half individually (in which
case you'll end up with two separate MMCs — or you can reassemble the
frosted halves to create a layered MMC). Decorate, if you wish, with semi-
sweet chocolate chips.

Molasses Microwave Mug Cake

INGREDIENTS
1 egg
1 tablespoon molasses
2 tablespoons oil
1/8 teaspoon vanilla extract
1/8 teaspoon baking powder
1/4 teaspoon ginger
4 tablespoons light brown sugar
2 tablespoons instant vanilla
pudding powder (not prepared)
4 tablespoons all-purpose flour
2 tablespoons of raisins (optional)

NOTE
Molasses on the table. Hold your tongue while you say that. (Well, it was funny when we were about six.)

DIRECTIONS
Prepare mug by coating the inside lightly with cooking spray.

Mix the ingredients in a small bowl. Beat egg first with a spoon and mix in other liquid ingredients. Then add dry ingredients and mix until you've removed all the lumps.

Pour the batter into the mug (do not fill more than halfway) and smooth the top with a spoon. Thump mug firmly on the tabletop six times to remove excess air bubbles. Place mug on top of a microwavable small plate or saucer.

Bake for 3 - 4 minutes. Check for doneness by inserting a toothpick in the middle of the microwave mug cake and removing the toothpick. If the toothpick is dry, the MMC is done.

Wait 2 minutes, then run a butter knife along the inside of the mug, and tip the cake into plate. Position the mug cake so that the slightly rounded top is on top. Your microwave mug cake will now look like a slightly overgrown muffin.

FANCY STUFF
Frost the whole Molasses Microwave Mug Cake with whipped cream, or split the MMC in half, and frost each half individually (in which case you'll end up with two separate MMCs — or you can reassemble the frosted halves to create a layered MMC). Decorate, if you wish, with raisins.

Orange Cocoa Jellybean Microwave Mug Cake

INGREDIENTS

1 egg
3 tablespoons orange juice
2 tablespoons oil
4 tablespoons sugar
1/8 teaspoon vanilla extract
1/8 teaspoon baking powder
**2 tablespoons unsweetened
cocoa powder**
5 tablespoons all-purpose flour
**2 tablespoons jellybeans
(about 16, carefully cut in half)**

NOTE
*We went in search of the Easter
Bunny, and we found the Orange
Cocoa Jellybean Microwave Mug
Cake instead.*

DIRECTIONS

Prepare mug by coating the inside lightly with cooking spray.

Mix the ingredients in a small bowl. Beat egg first with a spoon and mix
in other liquid ingredients. Then add dry ingredients and mix until you've
removed all the lumps.

Pour the batter into the mug (do not fill more than halfway) and smooth the
top with a spoon. Thump mug firmly on the tabletop six times to remove
excess air bubbles. Place mug on top of a microwavable small plate or saucer.

Bake for 3 - 4 minutes. Check for doneness by inserting a toothpick in the
middle of the microwave mug cake and removing the toothpick. If the
toothpick is dry, the MMC is done.

Wait 2 minutes, then run a butter knife along the inside of the mug, and tip
the cake into plate. Position the mug cake so that the slightly rounded top
is on top. Your microwave mug cake will now look like a slightly overgrown
muffin.

FANCY STUFF

Frost the whole Orange Cocoa Jellybean Microwave Mug Cake with
chocolate frosting, or split the MMC in half, and frost each half individually (in
which case you'll end up with two separate MMCs — or you can reassemble
the frosted halves to create a layered MMC). Decorate, if you wish, with
jellybeans.

66 **101 Recipes for Microwave Mug Cakes:** Single-Serving Snacks in Less Than 10 Minutes

Orange Vanilla Microwave Mug Cake

INGREDIENTS

1 egg
3 tablespoons orange juice
2 tablespoon oil
1/8 teaspoon orange extract
 (or vanilla extract)
1/8 teaspoon baking powder
1/4 teaspoon cinnamon
4 tablespoons light brown sugar
2 tablespoons instant vanilla
 pudding powder (not prepared)
5 tablespoons all-purpose flour

NOTE
If you're looking for a snack to enjoy with your orange juice, then frankly, you're probably drinking the wrong stuff. Try milk instead. It goes way better with MMCs.

DIRECTIONS

Prepare mug by coating the inside lightly with cooking spray.

Mix the ingredients in a small bowl. Beat egg first with a spoon and mix in other liquid ingredients. Then add dry ingredients and mix until you've removed all the lumps.

Pour the batter into the mug (do not fill more than halfway) and smooth the top with a spoon. Thump mug firmly on the tabletop six times to remove excess air bubbles. Place mug on top of a microwavable small plate or saucer.

Bake for 3 - 4 minutes. Check for doneness by inserting a toothpick in the middle of the microwave mug cake and removing the toothpick. If the toothpick is dry, the MMC is done.

Wait 2 minutes, then run a butter knife along the inside of the mug, and tip the cake into plate. Position the mug cake so that the slightly rounded top is on top. Your microwave mug cake will now look like a slightly overgrown muffin.

FANCY STUFF

Frost the whole Orange Vanilla Microwave Mug Cake with orange marmalade, or split the MMC in half, and frost each half individually (in which case you'll end up with two separate MMCs — or you can reassemble the frosted halves to create a layered MMC). Decorate, if you wish, with powdered sugar.

Peach Butterscotch Microwave Mug Cake

INGREDIENTS
1 egg
1 tablespoon peach baby food
1 tablespoon oil
1/8 teaspoon vanilla extract
1/8 teaspoon baking powder
1/4 teaspoon cinnamon
4 tablespoons light brown sugar
2 tablespoons instant butterscotch
   pudding powder (not prepared)
4 tablespoons all-purpose flour

NOTE
We know of two full-grown adults who lived on little except baby food for about three weeks after they'd had their wisdom teeth removed. What was strange was that their gums were completely healed after the first two days. They just really like mushy, bland food.

DIRECTIONS
Prepare mug by coating the inside lightly with cooking spray.

Mix the ingredients in a small bowl. Beat egg first with a spoon and mix in other liquid ingredients. Then add dry ingredients and mix until you've removed all the lumps.

Pour the batter into the mug (do not fill more than halfway) and smooth the top with a spoon. Thump mug firmly on the tabletop six times to remove excess air bubbles. Place mug on top of a microwavable small plate or saucer.

Bake for 3 - 4 minutes. Check for doneness by inserting a toothpick in the middle of the microwave mug cake and removing the toothpick. If the toothpick is dry, the MMC is done.

Wait 2 minutes, then run a butter knife along the inside of the mug, and tip the cake into plate. Position the mug cake so that the slightly rounded top is on top. Your microwave mug cake will now look like a slightly overgrown muffin.

FANCY STUFF
Frost the whole Peach Butterscotch Microwave Mug Cake with peach yogurt or peach jelly, or split the MMC in half, and frost each half individually (in which case you'll end up with two separate MMCs — or you can reassemble the frosted halves to create a layered MMC). Decorate, if you wish, with sliced peaches (fresh or canned).

Peach Chip Chocolate Microwave Mug Cake

INGREDIENTS

1 egg
3 tablespoons milk
3 tablespoons oil
1/8 teaspoon vanilla extract
1/8 teaspoon baking powder
1/4 teaspoon cinnamon
4 tablespoons light brown sugar
2 tablespoons peach instant
    gelatin powder (not prepared)
4 tablespoons all-purpose flour
2 tablespoons white chocolate chips

NOTE

If your mom ever told you that eating gelatin would help you build strong bones, then she'd be gratified to hear you were making yourself a Peach Chip Chocolate Microwave Mug Cake. Can you imagine how gleeful she'd feel if you also ate some Brussels sprouts?

DIRECTIONS

Prepare mug by coating the inside lightly with cooking spray.

Mix the ingredients in a small bowl. Beat egg first with a spoon and mix in other liquid ingredients. Then add dry ingredients and mix until you've removed all the lumps.

Pour the batter into the mug (do not fill more than halfway) and smooth the top with a spoon. Thump mug firmly on the tabletop six times to remove excess air bubbles. Place mug on top of a microwavable small plate or saucer.

Bake for 3 - 4 minutes. Check for doneness by inserting a toothpick in the middle of the microwave mug cake and removing the toothpick. If the toothpick is dry, the MMC is done.

Wait 2 minutes, then run a butter knife along the inside of the mug, and tip the cake into plate. Position the mug cake so that the slightly rounded top is on top. Your microwave mug cake will now look like a slightly overgrown muffin.

FANCY STUFF

Frost the whole Peach Chip Chocolate Microwave Mug Cake with whipped cream, or split the MMC in half, and frost each half individually (in which case you'll end up with two separate MMCs — or you can reassemble the frosted halves to create a layered MMC). Decorate, if you wish, with white chocolate chips.

Peach Cobbler Microwave Mug Cake

INGREDIENTS
1 egg
1 tablespoon peach baby food
1 tablespoon oil
1/8 teaspoon vanilla extract
1/8 teaspoon baking powder
1/4 teaspoon cinnamon
4 tablespoons light brown sugar
2 tablespoons instant vanilla
   pudding powder (not prepared)
4 tablespoons all-purpose flour

NOTE
We know the cobbler's children seldom wear shoes. It makes us wonder whether they ever get to eat a Peach Cobbler Microwave Mug Cake.

DIRECTIONS
Prepare mug by coating the inside lightly with cooking spray.

Mix the ingredients in a small bowl. Beat egg first with a spoon and mix in other liquid ingredients. Then add dry ingredients and mix until you've removed all the lumps.

Pour the batter into the mug (do not fill more than halfway) and smooth the top with a spoon. Thump mug firmly on the tabletop six times to remove excess air bubbles. Place mug on top of a microwavable small plate or saucer.

Bake for 3 - 4 minutes. Check for doneness by inserting a toothpick in the middle of the microwave mug cake and removing the toothpick. If the toothpick is dry, the MMC is done.

Wait 2 minutes, then run a butter knife along the inside of the mug, and tip the cake into plate. Position the mug cake so that the slightly rounded top is on top. Your microwave mug cake will now look like a slightly overgrown muffin.

FANCY STUFF
Frost the whole Peach Cobbler Microwave Mug Cake with peach yogurt or peach jelly, or split the MMC in half, and frost each half individually (in which case you'll end up with two separate MMCs — or you can reassemble the frosted halves to create a layered MMC). Decorate, if you wish, with small candies, or with sliced peaches (fresh or canned).

Peach Mango Strawberry Microwave Mug Cake

INGREDIENTS

1 egg
**2 tablespoons mixed strawberry
yogurt (with the fruit stirred in)**
1 tablespoon oil
1/8 teaspoon vanilla extract
1/8 teaspoon baking powder
1/4 teaspoon cinnamon
4 tablespoons light brown sugar
**1 tablespoon Green Tea Peach
Mango Crystal Light powder
(that's one individual package)**
5 tablespoons all-purpose flour

NOTE

We've been entranced by Crystal Light from the first time we saw our friend, Evvie, tear open an envelope at our favorite restaurant and turn her ice water a dazzling shade of orange. If you haven't yet had the experience, don't fret. We're sure Evvie would be delighted to join you for lunch sometime, too.

DIRECTIONS

Prepare mug by coating the inside lightly with cooking spray.

Mix the ingredients in a small bowl. Beat egg first with a spoon and mix in other liquid ingredients. Then add dry ingredients and mix until you've removed all the lumps.

Pour the batter into the mug (do not fill more than halfway) and smooth the top with a spoon. Thump mug firmly on the tabletop six times to remove excess air bubbles. Place mug on top of a microwavable small plate or saucer.

Bake for 3 - 4 minutes. Check for doneness by inserting a toothpick in the middle of the microwave mug cake and removing the toothpick. If the toothpick is dry, the MMC is done.

Wait 2 minutes, then run a butter knife along the inside of the mug, and tip the cake into plate. Position the mug cake so that the slightly rounded top is on top. Your microwave mug cake will now look like a slightly overgrown muffin.

FANCY STUFF

Frost the whole Peach Mango Strawberry Microwave Mug Cake with strawberry jelly, or the rest of the strawberry yogurt, or split the MMC in half, and frost each half individually (in which case you'll end up with two separate MMCs — or you can reassemble the frosted halves to create a layered MMC). Decorate, if you wish, with fresh or frozen strawberries.

Peanut Butter and Banana Microwave Mug Cake

INGREDIENTS
1 egg
1 tablespoon banana baby food
1 tablespoon peanut butter
  (smooth or chunky)
2 tablespoons oil
1/8 teaspoon vanilla extract
1/8 teaspoon baking powder
1/4 teaspoon cinnamon
4 tablespoons light brown sugar
2 tablespoons instant banana
  pudding powder (not prepared)
4 tablespoons all-purpose flour

NOTE
One word comes to mind when we think of peanut butter and bananas: indigestion. Others, some of our intrepid MMC testers also think of Elvis.

DIRECTIONS
Prepare mug by coating the inside lightly with cooking spray.

Mix the ingredients in a small bowl. Beat egg first with a spoon and mix in other liquid ingredients. Then add dry ingredients and mix until you've removed all the lumps.

Pour the batter into the mug (do not fill more than halfway) and smooth the top with a spoon. Thump mug firmly on the tabletop six times to remove excess air bubbles. Place mug on top of a microwavable small plate or saucer.

Bake for 3 - 4 minutes. Check for doneness by inserting a toothpick in the middle of the microwave mug cake and removing the toothpick. If the toothpick is dry, the MMC is done.

Wait 2 minutes, then run a butter knife along the inside of the mug, and tip the cake into plate. Position the mug cake so that the slightly rounded top is on top. Your microwave mug cake will now look like a slightly overgrown muffin.

FANCY STUFF
Frost the whole Peanut Butter and Banana Microwave Mug Cake with peanut butter or whipped cream, or split the MMC in half, and frost each half individually (in which case you'll end up with two separate MMCs — or you can reassemble the frosted halves to create a layered MMC). Decorate, if you wish, with sliced bananas (fresh or dried).

Peanut Butter and Jelly Microwave Mug Cake

INGREDIENTS
1 egg
1 tablespoon grape jelly
1 tablespoon peanut butter
  (smooth or chunky)
2 tablespoons oil
1/8 teaspoon vanilla extract
1/8 teaspoon baking powder
1/4 teaspoon cinnamon
4 tablespoons light brown sugar
2 tablespoons instant vanilla
  pudding powder (not prepared)
4 tablespoons all-purpose flour

NOTE
Do grapes have to apply for membership in the jelly club, and if so, what is the fee?

DIRECTIONS
Prepare mug by coating the inside lightly with cooking spray.

Mix the ingredients in a small bowl. Beat egg first with a spoon and mix in other liquid ingredients. Then add dry ingredients and mix until you've removed all the lumps.

Pour the batter into the mug (do not fill more than halfway) and smooth the top with a spoon. Thump mug firmly on the tabletop six times to remove excess air bubbles. Place mug on top of a microwavable small plate or saucer.

Bake for 3 - 4 minutes. Check for doneness by inserting a toothpick in the middle of the microwave mug cake and removing the toothpick. If the toothpick is dry, the MMC is done.

Wait 2 minutes, then run a butter knife along the inside of the mug, and tip the cake into plate. Position the mug cake so that the slightly rounded top is on top. Your microwave mug cake will now look like a slightly overgrown muffin.

FANCY STUFF
Frost the whole Peanut Butter and Jelly Microwave Mug Cake with peanut butter or grape jelly, or split the MMC in half, and frost each half individually (in which case you'll end up with two separate MMCs — or you can reassemble the frosted halves to create a layered MMC). Decorate, if you wish, with small candies such as gumdrops or jellybeans.

Pineapple Chocolate Microwave Mug Cake

INGREDIENTS

1 egg
3 tablespoons milk
2 tablespoons oil
1/8 teaspoon vanilla extract
1/8 teaspoon baking powder
4 tablespoons sugar
2 tablespoons instant chocolate
pudding powder (not prepared)
4 tablespoons all-purpose flour
2 tablespoons crushed pineapple
(with the juice drained out)

NOTE
Why did our team of intrepid MMC testers feel the need to drop their pineapples out of a seven-story window in order to get crushed pineapple?

DIRECTIONS

Prepare mug by coating the inside lightly with cooking spray.

Mix the ingredients in a small bowl. Beat egg first with a spoon and mix in other liquid ingredients. Then add dry ingredients and mix until you've removed all the lumps.

Pour the batter into the mug (do not fill more than halfway) and smooth the top with a spoon. Thump mug firmly on the tabletop six times to remove excess air bubbles. Place mug on top of a microwavable small plate or saucer.

Bake for 3 - 4 minutes. Check for doneness by inserting a toothpick in the middle of the microwave mug cake and removing the toothpick. If the toothpick is dry, the MMC is done.

Wait 2 minutes, then run a butter knife along the inside of the mug, and tip the cake into plate. Position the mug cake so that the slightly rounded top is on top. Your microwave mug cake will now look like a slightly overgrown muffin.

FANCY STUFF

Frost the whole Pineapple Chocolate Microwave Mug Cake with chocolate frosting or pineapple yogurt, or split the MMC in half, and frost each half individually (in which case you'll end up with two separate MMCs — or you can reassemble the frosted halves to create a layered MMC). Decorate, if you wish, with crushed pineapple (with the juice drained out).

Pineapple Peach Microwave Mug Cake

INGREDIENTS

1 egg

2 tablespoons mixed pineapple
   yogurt (with the fruit stirred in)

1 tablespoon oil

1/8 teaspoon vanilla extract

1/8 teaspoon baking powder

1/4 teaspoon cinnamon

4 tablespoons light brown sugar

1 tablespoon Peach Tea Crystal
   Light powder (that's one
   individual package)

5 tablespoons all-purpose flour

NOTE
*Have you heard of the Pineapple
Peach Ranch? Neither have we.*

DIRECTIONS

Prepare mug by coating the inside lightly with cooking spray.

Mix the ingredients in a small bowl. Beat egg first with a spoon and mix
in other liquid ingredients. Then add dry ingredients and mix until you've
removed all the lumps.

Pour the batter into the mug (do not fill more than halfway) and smooth the
top with a spoon. Thump mug firmly on the tabletop six times to remove
excess air bubbles. Place mug on top of a microwavable small plate or saucer.

Bake for 3 - 4 minutes. Check for doneness by inserting a toothpick in the
middle of the microwave mug cake and removing the toothpick. If the
toothpick is dry, the MMC is done.

Wait 2 minutes, then run a butter knife along the inside of the mug, and tip
the cake into plate. Position the mug cake so that the slightly rounded top
is on top. Your microwave mug cake will now look like a slightly overgrown
muffin.

FANCY STUFF

Frost the whole Pineapple Peach Microwave Mug Cake with pineapple
yogurt, or split the MMC in half, and frost each half individually (in which case
you'll end up with two separate MMCs — or you can reassemble the frosted
halves to create a layered MMC). Decorate, if you wish, with peach slices (fresh
or canned).

Pineapple Pistachio Microwave Mug Cake

INGREDIENTS

1 egg
2 tablespoons pineapple yogurt (with the fruit stirred in)
1 tablespoon oil
1/8 teaspoon vanilla extract
1/8 teaspoon baking powder
1/4 teaspoon cinnamon
4 tablespoons light brown sugar
2 tablespoons instant pistachio pudding powder (not prepared)
4 tablespoons all-purpose flour

NOTE
We once spent an hour opening up pistachio nuts, and our fingers turned red. Why, then, is pistachio pudding green? That may be one of the great mysteries of life.

DIRECTIONS

Prepare mug by coating the inside lightly with cooking spray.

Mix the ingredients in a small bowl. Beat egg first with a spoon and mix in other liquid ingredients. Then add dry ingredients and mix until you've removed all the lumps.

Pour the batter into the mug (do not fill more than halfway) and smooth the top with a spoon. Thump mug firmly on the tabletop six times to remove excess air bubbles. Place mug on top of a microwavable small plate or saucer.

Bake for 3 - 4 minutes. Check for doneness by inserting a toothpick in the middle of the microwave mug cake and removing the toothpick. If the toothpick is dry, the MMC is done.

Wait 2 minutes, then run a butter knife along the inside of the mug, and tip the cake into plate. Position the mug cake so that the slightly rounded top is on top. Your microwave mug cake will now look like a slightly overgrown muffin.

FANCY STUFF

Frost the whole Pineapple Pistachio Microwave Mug Cake with pineapple yogurt, or split the MMC in half, and frost each half individually (in which case you'll end up with two separate MMCs — or you can reassemble the frosted halves to create a layered MMC). Decorate, if you wish, with small gumdrops, jellybeans, or pistachio nuts.

Pizza Microwave Mug Cake

INGREDIENTS
1 egg
2 tablespoons spaghetti sauce
2 tablespoons oil
1/8 teaspoon vanilla extract
1/8 teaspoon baking powder
1/8 teaspoon salt
1 tablespoon light brown sugar
**2 tablespoons instant vanilla
   pudding powder (not prepared)**
**3 tablespoons shredded
   mozzarella cheese**
5 tablespoons all-purpose flour

NOTE
*When given the recipe for the
Pizza Microwave Mug Cake,
one of our intrepid MMC testers
gushed, "Oh! I'm going to add
pineapple chunks to mine!" We
regret to say that, to the best of
our knowledge, she was serious.*

DIRECTIONS
Prepare mug by coating the inside lightly with cooking spray.

Mix the ingredients in a small bowl. Beat egg first with a spoon and mix
in other liquid ingredients. Then add dry ingredients and mix until you've
removed all the lumps.

Pour the batter into the mug (do not fill more than halfway) and smooth the
top with a spoon. Thump mug firmly on the tabletop six times to remove
excess air bubbles. Place mug on top of a microwavable small plate or saucer.

Bake for 3 - 4 minutes. Check for doneness by inserting a toothpick in the
middle of the microwave mug cake and removing the toothpick. If the
toothpick is dry, the MMC is done.

Wait 2 minutes, then run a butter knife along the inside of the mug, and tip
the cake into plate. Position the mug cake so that the slightly rounded top
is on top. Your microwave mug cake will now look like a slightly overgrown
muffin.

FANCY STUFF
Sprinkle the whole Pizza Microwave Mug Cake with shredded mozzarella
cheese, or split the MMC in half, and sprinkle each half with shredded
mozzarella cheese individually (in which case you'll end up with two separate
Pizza Microwave Mug Cakes — or you can reassemble the cheese-topped
halves to create a layer Pizza MMC). Decorate, if you wish, with pepperoni
slices.

Pruney Raisin Microwave Mug Cake

INGREDIENTS

1 egg
1 tablespoon prune baby food
1 tablespoon oil
1/8 teaspoon baking powder
1/8 teaspoon vanilla extract
4 tablespoons sugar
1 tablespoon unsweetened
cocoa powder
4 tablespoons all-purpose flour
2 tablespoons raisins

NOTE
Focus on prunes for a moment.
How does that make you feel?
Sorry, the restroom is occupied
right now.

DIRECTIONS

Prepare mug by coating the inside lightly with cooking spray.

Mix the ingredients in a small bowl. Beat egg first with a spoon and mix in other liquid ingredients. Then add dry ingredients and mix until you've removed all the lumps.

Pour the batter into the mug (do not fill more than halfway) and smooth the top with a spoon. Thump mug firmly on the tabletop six times to remove excess air bubbles. Place mug on top of a microwavable small plate or saucer.

Bake for 3 - 4 minutes. Check for doneness by inserting a toothpick in the middle of the microwave mug cake and removing the toothpick. If the toothpick is dry, the MMC is done.

Wait 2 minutes, then run a butter knife along the inside of the mug, and tip the cake into plate. Position the mug cake so that the slightly rounded top is on top. Your microwave mug cake will now look like a slightly overgrown muffin.

FANCY STUFF

Frost the whole Pruney Raisin Microwave Mug Cake with whipped cream, or split the MMC in half, and frost each half individually (in which case you'll end up with two separate MMCs — or you can reassemble the frosted halves to create a layered MMC). Decorate, if you wish, with dried raisins.

Pumpkin Pie Microwave Mug Cake

INGREDIENTS

1 egg
1 tablespoon pumpkin
  pie filling
1 tablespoon oil
1/8 teaspoon vanilla extract
1/8 teaspoon baking powder
1/2 teaspoon cinnamon
1/4 teaspoon nutmeg
1/4 teaspoon ginger
4 tablespoons light brown sugar
2 tablespoons instant vanilla
  pudding powder (not prepared)
4 tablespoons all-purpose flour

NOTE
If you truly hate those holiday time family get-togethers, then why not spend your next Thanksgiving in the kitchen making all the relatives their own MMCs?

DIRECTIONS

Prepare mug by coating the inside lightly with cooking spray.

Mix the ingredients in a small bowl. Beat egg first with a spoon and mix in other liquid ingredients. Then add dry ingredients and mix until you've removed all the lumps.

Pour the batter into the mug (do not fill more than halfway) and smooth the top with a spoon. Thump mug firmly on the tabletop six times to remove excess air bubbles. Place mug on top of a microwavable small plate or saucer.

Bake for 3 - 4 minutes. Check for doneness by inserting a toothpick in the middle of the microwave mug cake and removing the toothpick. If the toothpick is dry, the MMC is done.

Wait 2 minutes, then run a butter knife along the inside of the mug, and tip the cake into plate. Position the mug cake so that the slightly rounded top is on top. Your microwave mug cake will now look like a slightly overgrown muffin.

FANCY STUFF

Frost the whole Pumpkin Pie Microwave Mug Cake with whipped cream, or split the MMC in half, and frost each half individually (in which case you'll end up with two separate MMCs — or you can reassemble the frosted halves to create a layered MMC). Decorate, if you wish, with candied ginger or cinnamon.

Punky's Dilemma Microwave Mug Cake

INGREDIENTS

1 egg
2 tablespoons boysenberry
yogurt (with the fruit stirred in)
1 tablespoon oil
1/8 teaspoon vanilla extract
1/8 teaspoon baking powder
1/4 teaspoon cinnamon
4 tablespoons light brown sugar
2 tablespoons instant vanilla
pudding powder (not prepared)
4 tablespoons all-purpose flour

NOTE
We bought our first container of boysenberry jam as a homage to Paul Simon and Art Garfunkel. We hope they got a commission.

DIRECTIONS

Prepare mug by coating the inside lightly with cooking spray.

Mix the ingredients in a small bowl. Beat egg first with a spoon and mix in other liquid ingredients. Then add dry ingredients and mix until you've removed all the lumps.

Pour the batter into the mug (do not fill more than halfway) and smooth the top with a spoon. Thump mug firmly on the tabletop six times to remove excess air bubbles. Place mug on top of a microwavable small plate or saucer.

Bake for 3 - 4 minutes. Check for doneness by inserting a toothpick in the middle of the microwave mug cake and removing the toothpick. If the toothpick is dry, the MMC is done.

Wait 2 minutes, then run a butter knife along the inside of the mug, and tip the cake into plate. Position the mug cake so that the slightly rounded top is on top. Your microwave mug cake will now look like a slightly overgrown muffin.

FANCY STUFF

Frost the whole Punky's Dilemma Microwave Mug Cake with boysenberry yogurt or boysenberry jam, or split the MMC in half, and frost each half individually (in which case you'll end up with two separate MMCs — or you can reassemble the frosted halves to create a layered MMC). Decorate, if you wish, with small candies such as gumdrops or jellybeans.

Raspberriest Microwave Mug Cake

INGREDIENTS
1 egg
1 tablespoon raspberry baby food
1 tablespoon oil
1/8 teaspoon vanilla extract
1/8 teaspoon baking powder
1/4 teaspoon cinnamon
4 tablespoons light brown sugar
2 tablespoons raspberry instant
  gelatin powder (not prepared)
4 tablespoons all-purpose flour

NOTE
We just have this to say to people who don't love the Raspberriest Microwave Mug Cake: phhhhhhbbbbtttttt!!!

DIRECTIONS
Prepare mug by coating the inside lightly with cooking spray.

Mix the ingredients in a small bowl. Beat egg first with a spoon and mix in other liquid ingredients. Then add dry ingredients and mix until you've removed all the lumps.

Pour the batter into the mug (do not fill more than halfway) and smooth the top with a spoon. Thump mug firmly on the tabletop six times to remove excess air bubbles. Place mug on top of a microwavable small plate or saucer.

Bake for 3 - 4 minutes. Check for doneness by inserting a toothpick in the middle of the microwave mug cake and removing the toothpick. If the toothpick is dry, the MMC is done.

Wait 2 minutes, then run a butter knife along the inside of the mug, and tip the cake into plate. Position the mug cake so that the slightly rounded top is on top. Your microwave mug cake will now look like a slightly overgrown muffin.

FANCY STUFF
Frost the whole Raspberriest Microwave Mug Cake with raspberry yogurt or raspberry jelly, or split the MMC in half, and frost each half individually (in which case you'll end up with two separate MMCs — or you can reassemble the frosted halves to create a layered MMC). Decorate, if you wish, with fresh or frozen raspberries.

Rascranberry Microwave Mug Cake

INGREDIENTS

1 egg
3 tablespoons cranberry juice
2 tablespoons oil
1/8 teaspoon vanilla extract
1/8 teaspoon baking powder
4 tablespoons light brown sugar
2 tablespoons raspberry instant
  gelatin powder (not prepared)
5 tablespoons all-purpose flour
2 tablespoons dried cranberries

NOTE
If you're hooked on those dried cranberries, you should know they come in no-sugar-added varieties, too. We're sorry we had to break the bad news to you.

DIRECTIONS

Prepare mug by coating the inside lightly with cooking spray.

Mix the ingredients in a small bowl. Beat egg first with a spoon and mix in other liquid ingredients. Then add dry ingredients and mix until you've removed all the lumps.

Pour the batter into the mug (do not fill more than halfway) and smooth the top with a spoon. Thump mug firmly on the tabletop six times to remove excess air bubbles. Place mug on top of a microwavable small plate or saucer.

Bake for 3 - 4 minutes. Check for doneness by inserting a toothpick in the middle of the microwave mug cake and removing the toothpick. If the toothpick is dry, the MMC is done.

Wait 2 minutes, then run a butter knife along the inside of the mug, and tip the cake into plate. Position the mug cake so that the slightly rounded top is on top. Your microwave mug cake will now look like a slightly overgrown muffin.

FANCY STUFF

Frost the whole Rascranberry Microwave Mug Cake with whipped cream, or split the MMC in half, and frost each half individually (in which case you'll end up with two separate MMCs — or you can reassemble the frosted halves to create a layered MMC). Decorate, if you wish, with fresh or frozen raspberries.

S'More Microwave Mug Cake

INGREDIENTS

1 egg
3 tablespoons milk
3 tablespoons oil
1/8 teaspoon vanilla extract
1/8 teaspoon baking powder
4 tablespoons sugar
2 tablespoons unsweetened
  cocoa powder
1 tablespoon graham cracker crumbs
4 tablespoons all-purpose flour

NOTE
Remember standing around the campfire making s'mores? Well, making the S'More Microwave Mug Cake is nothing like that.

DIRECTIONS

Prepare mug by coating the inside lightly with cooking spray.

Mix the ingredients in a small bowl. Beat egg first with a spoon and mix in other liquid ingredients. Then add dry ingredients and mix until you've removed all the lumps.

Pour the batter into the mug (do not fill more than halfway) and smooth the top with a spoon. Thump mug firmly on the tabletop six times to remove excess air bubbles. Place mug on top of a microwavable small plate or saucer.

Bake for 3 - 4 minutes. Check for doneness by inserting a toothpick in the middle of the microwave mug cake and removing the toothpick. If the toothpick is dry, the MMC is done.

Wait 2 minutes, then run a butter knife along the inside of the mug, and tip the cake into plate. Position the mug cake so that the slightly rounded top is on top. Your microwave mug cake will now look like a slightly overgrown muffin.

FANCY STUFF

Frost the whole S'More Microwave Mug Cake with marshmallow cream, or split the MMC in half, and frost each half individually (in which case you'll end up with two separate MMCs — or you can reassemble the frosted halves to create a layered MMC). Decorate, if you wish, with miniature marshmallows.

Snowball Microwave Mug Cake

INGREDIENTS

1 egg
1 tablespoon strawberry
  pie filling
1 tablespoon oil
1/8 teaspoon coconut extract
  (or vanilla extract)
1/8 teaspoon baking powder
4 tablespoons sugar
2 tablespoons strawberry-flavored
  NESQUIK®
4 tablespoons all-purpose flour
2 tablespoons shredded coconut

NOTE
*Many snowballs living in Florida
have never seen the beach.*

DIRECTIONS

Prepare mug by coating the inside lightly with cooking spray.

Mix the ingredients in a small bowl. Beat egg first with a spoon and mix
in other liquid ingredients. Then add dry ingredients and mix until you've
removed all the lumps.

Pour the batter into the mug (do not fill more than halfway) and smooth the
top with a spoon. Thump mug firmly on the tabletop six times to remove
excess air bubbles. Place mug on top of a microwavable small plate or saucer.

Bake for 3 - 4 minutes. Check for doneness by inserting a toothpick in the
middle of the microwave mug cake and removing the toothpick. If the
toothpick is dry, the MMC is done.

Wait 2 minutes, then run a butter knife along the inside of the mug, and tip
the cake into plate. Position the mug cake so that the slightly rounded top
is on top. Your microwave mug cake will now look like a slightly overgrown
muffin.

FANCY STUFF

Frost the whole Snowball Microwave Mug Cake with strawberry jelly, or split
the MMC in half, and frost each half individually (in which case you'll end
up with two separate MMCs — or you can reassemble the frosted halves to
create a layered MMC). Decorate, if you wish, with shredded coconut.

Spicy Squash Microwave Mug Cake

INGREDIENTS
1 egg
1 tablespoon squash baby food
1 tablespoon oil
1/8 teaspoon vanilla extract
1/8 teaspoon baking powder
1/4 teaspoon cinnamon
1/8 teaspoon nutmeg
1/8 teaspoon cloves
4 tablespoons light brown sugar
2 tablespoons instant vanilla
  pudding powder (not prepared)
4 tablespoons all-purpose flour

NOTE
If you squish a jar of squash baby food, does anything happen?

DIRECTIONS
Prepare mug by coating the inside lightly with cooking spray.

Mix the ingredients in a small bowl. Beat egg first with a spoon and mix in other liquid ingredients. Then add dry ingredients and mix until you've removed all the lumps.

Pour the batter into the mug (do not fill more than halfway) and smooth the top with a spoon. Thump mug firmly on the tabletop six times to remove excess air bubbles. Place mug on top of a microwavable small plate or saucer.

Bake for 3 - 4 minutes. Check for doneness by inserting a toothpick in the middle of the microwave mug cake and removing the toothpick. If the toothpick is dry, the MMC is done.

Wait 2 minutes, then run a butter knife along the inside of the mug, and tip the cake into plate. Position the mug cake so that the slightly rounded top is on top. Your microwave mug cake will now look like a slightly overgrown muffin.

FANCY STUFF
Frost the whole Spicy Squash Microwave Mug Cake with cream cheese frosting or just plain cream cheese, or split the MMC in half, and frost each half individually (in which case you'll end up with two separate MMCs — or you can reassemble the frosted halves to create a layered MMC). Decorate, if you wish, with small candies such as gumdrops or jellybeans.

Strawberry and Chocolate Chip Microwave Mug Cake

INGREDIENTS

1 egg
3 tablespoons milk
3 tablespoons oil
1/8 teaspoon vanilla extract
1/8 teaspoon baking powder
1/4 teaspoon cinnamon
4 tablespoons light brown sugar
2 tablespoons strawberry-flavored
  NESQUIK®
4 tablespoons all-purpose flour
2 tablespoons semi-sweet
  chocolate chips

NOTE
Why doesn't someone invent strawberries with chocolate chips already in them? Everyone would buy some of those plants!

DIRECTIONS

Prepare mug by coating the inside lightly with cooking spray.

Mix the ingredients in a small bowl. Beat egg first with a spoon and mix in other liquid ingredients. Then add dry ingredients and mix until you've removed all the lumps.

Pour the batter into the mug (do not fill more than halfway) and smooth the top with a spoon. Thump mug firmly on the tabletop six times to remove excess air bubbles. Place mug on top of a microwavable small plate or saucer.

Bake for 3 - 4 minutes. Check for doneness by inserting a toothpick in the middle of the microwave mug cake and removing the toothpick. If the toothpick is dry, the MMC is done.

Wait 2 minutes, then run a butter knife along the inside of the mug, and tip the cake into plate. Position the mug cake so that the slightly rounded top is on top. Your microwave mug cake will now look like a slightly overgrown muffin.

FANCY STUFF

Frost the whole Strawberry and Chocolate Chip Microwave Mug Cake with chocolate frosting, or split the MMC in half, and frost each half individually (in which case you'll end up with two separate MMCs — or you can reassemble the frosted halves to create a layered MMC). Decorate, if you wish, with semi-sweet chocolate chips.

Strawberry Banana Pistachio Microwave Mug Cake

INGREDIENTS

1 egg
2 tablespoons strawberry
  and banana yogurt
  (with the fruit stirred in)
1 tablespoon oil
1/8 teaspoon vanilla extract
1/8 teaspoon baking powder
1/4 teaspoon cinnamon
4 tablespoons light brown sugar
2 tablespoons instant pistachio
  pudding powder (not prepared)
4 tablespoons all-purpose flour

NOTE
Imagine how cool it would be if you could peel a strawberry. Or hull a banana.

DIRECTIONS

Prepare mug by coating the inside lightly with cooking spray.

Mix the ingredients in a small bowl. Beat egg first with a spoon and mix in other liquid ingredients. Then add dry ingredients and mix until you've removed all the lumps.

Pour the batter into the mug (do not fill more than halfway) and smooth the top with a spoon. Thump mug firmly on the tabletop six times to remove excess air bubbles. Place mug on top of a microwavable small plate or saucer.

Bake for 3 - 4 minutes. Check for doneness by inserting a toothpick in the middle of the microwave mug cake and removing the toothpick. If the toothpick is dry, the MMC is done.

Wait 2 minutes, then run a butter knife along the inside of the mug, and tip the cake into plate. Position the mug cake so that the slightly rounded top is on top. Your microwave mug cake will now look like a slightly overgrown muffin.

FANCY STUFF

Frost the whole Strawberry Banana Pistachio Microwave Mug Cake with strawberry and banana yogurt, or split the MMC in half, and frost each half individually (in which case you'll end up with two separate MMCs — or you can reassemble the frosted halves to create a layered MMC). Decorate, if you wish, with fresh or frozen strawberries or pistachio nuts.

Strawberry Cheesecake Microwave Mug Cake

INGREDIENTS

1 egg
1 tablespoon softened cream cheese
1 tablespoon ricotta cheese
2 tablespoons oil
1/8 teaspoon vanilla extract
1/8 teaspoon baking powder
1/4 teaspoon cinnamon
4 tablespoons light brown sugar
1 tablespoon strawberry-flavored NESQUIK®
1 tablespoon graham cracker crumbs
4 tablespoons all-purpose flour

NOTE
How many graham crackers do you suppose you'd have to eat before you generate enough crumbs to equal one tablespoon? Just kidding. They sell boxes of crumbs. Who gets paid to eat all those graham crackers, anyway?

DIRECTIONS

Prepare mug by coating the inside lightly with cooking spray.

Mix the ingredients in a small bowl. Beat egg first with a spoon and mix in other liquid ingredients. Then add dry ingredients and mix until you've removed all the lumps.

Pour the batter into the mug (do not fill more than halfway) and smooth the top with a spoon. Thump mug firmly on the tabletop six times to remove excess air bubbles. Place mug on top of a microwavable small plate or saucer.

Bake for 3 - 4 minutes. Check for doneness by inserting a toothpick in the middle of the microwave mug cake and removing the toothpick. If the toothpick is dry, the MMC is done.

Wait 2 minutes, then run a butter knife along the inside of the mug, and tip the cake into plate. Position the mug cake so that the slightly rounded top is on top. Your microwave mug cake will now look like a slightly overgrown muffin.

FANCY STUFF

Frost the whole Strawberry Cheesecake Microwave Mug Cake with chocolate or cream cheese frosting, or split the MMC in half, and frost each half individually (in which case you'll end up with two separate MMCs — or you can reassemble the frosted halves to create a layered MMC). Decorate, if you wish, with graham cracker crumbs or strawberries.

Strawberry Honey Raisin Microwave Mug Cake

INGREDIENTS
1 egg
2 tablespoons honey
2 tablespoons oil
1/8 teaspoon vanilla extract
1/8 teaspoon baking powder
1/4 teaspoon cinnamon
2 tablespoons light brown sugar
**4 tablespoons strawberry-flavored
  NESQUIK®**
4 tablespoons all-purpose flour
2 tablespoons raisins

NOTE
Sure, you can substitute cinnamon chips for raisins, if you'd prefer, but think about how many raisins you'd put out of work. Could you really live with yourself?

DIRECTIONS
Prepare mug by coating the inside lightly with cooking spray.

Mix the ingredients in a small bowl. Beat egg first with a spoon and mix in other liquid ingredients. Then add dry ingredients and mix until you've removed all the lumps.

Pour the batter into the mug (do not fill more than halfway) and smooth the top with a spoon. Thump mug firmly on the tabletop six times to remove excess air bubbles. Place mug on top of a microwavable small plate or saucer.

Bake for 3 - 4 minutes. Check for doneness by inserting a toothpick in the middle of the microwave mug cake and removing the toothpick. If the toothpick is dry, the MMC is done.

Wait 2 minutes, then run a butter knife along the inside of the mug, and tip the cake into plate. Position the mug cake so that the slightly rounded top is on top. Your microwave mug cake will now look like a slightly overgrown muffin.

FANCY STUFF
Frost the whole Strawberry Honey Raisin Microwave Mug Cake with whipped cream, or split the MMC in half, and frost each half individually (in which case you'll end up with two separate MMCs — or you can reassemble the frosted halves to create a layered MMC). Decorate, if you wish, with fresh or frozen strawberries.

Strawberry Kiwi Lemon Microwave Mug Cake

INGREDIENTS
1 egg
2 tablespoons lemon yogurt
1 tablespoon oil
1/8 teaspoon vanilla extract
1/8 teaspoon baking powder
1/4 teaspoon cinnamon
4 tablespoons light brown sugar
1 tablespoon Strawberry Kiwi
   Crystal Light powder
   (that's one individual package)
5 tablespoons all-purpose flour

NOTE
Lemon was the first flavored yogurt we ever tried, and it's still the best there is. So why squander any on a Strawberry Kiwi Lemon Microwave Mug Cake? That's something we struggle with.

DIRECTIONS
Prepare mug by coating the inside lightly with cooking spray.

Mix the ingredients in a small bowl. Beat egg first with a spoon and mix in other liquid ingredients. Then add dry ingredients and mix until you've removed all the lumps.

Pour the batter into the mug (do not fill more than halfway) and smooth the top with a spoon. Thump mug firmly on the tabletop six times to remove excess air bubbles. Place mug on top of a microwavable small plate or saucer.

Bake for 3 - 4 minutes. Check for doneness by inserting a toothpick in the middle of the microwave mug cake and removing the toothpick. If the toothpick is dry, the MMC is done.

Wait 2 minutes, then run a butter knife along the inside of the mug, and tip the cake into plate. Position the mug cake so that the slightly rounded top is on top. Your microwave mug cake will now look like a slightly overgrown muffin.

FANCY STUFF
Frost the whole Strawberry Kiwi Lemon Microwave Mug Cake with lemon yogurt or lemon pie filling, or the rest of the lemon yogurt, or split the MMC in half, and frost each half individually (in which case you'll end up with two separate MMCs — or you can reassemble the frosted halves to create a layered MMC). Decorate, if you wish, with fresh or frozen strawberries.

Strawberry Pineapple Microwave Mug Cake

INGREDIENTS
1 egg
2 tablespoons pineapple yogurt
  (with the fruit stirred in)
1 tablespoon oil
1/8 teaspoon vanilla extract
1/8 teaspoon baking powder
1/4 teaspoon cinnamon
4 tablespoons light brown sugar
2 tablespoons strawberry-flavored
  NESQUIK®
4 tablespoons all-purpose flour

NOTE
Imagine how great pineapple chunks would taste if you dipped them into some of that strawberry-flavored drink mix powder. Too bad you can't also try dunking your fortune cookies.

DIRECTIONS
Prepare mug by coating the inside lightly with cooking spray.

Mix the ingredients in a small bowl. Beat egg first with a spoon and mix in other liquid ingredients. Then add dry ingredients and mix until you've removed all the lumps.

Pour the batter into the mug (do not fill more than halfway) and smooth the top with a spoon. Thump mug firmly on the tabletop six times to remove excess air bubbles. Place mug on top of a microwavable small plate or saucer.

Bake for 3 - 4 minutes. Check for doneness by inserting a toothpick in the middle of the microwave mug cake and removing the toothpick. If the toothpick is dry, the MMC is done.

Wait 2 minutes, then run a butter knife along the inside of the mug, and tip the cake into plate. Position the mug cake so that the slightly rounded top is on top. Your microwave mug cake will now look like a slightly overgrown muffin.

FANCY STUFF
Frost the whole Strawberry Pineapple Microwave Mug Cake with whipped cream, or split the MMC in half, and frost each half individually (in which case you'll end up with two separate MMCs — or you can reassemble the frosted halves to create a layered MMC). Decorate, if you wish, with pineapple chunks or strawberries.

Tapioca Microwave Mug Cake

INGREDIENTS

1 egg
3 tablespoons milk
3 tablespoons oil
1/8 teaspoon vanilla extract
1/8 teaspoon baking powder
1/4 teaspoon cinnamon
4 tablespoons light brown sugar
**2 tablespoons instant tapioca
  pudding powder (not prepared)**
4 tablespoons all-purpose flour

NOTE
*Does tapioca pudding wear taps
on its dancing shoes, or is there a
whole other reason for its name?*

DIRECTIONS

Prepare mug by coating the inside lightly with cooking spray.

Mix the ingredients in a small bowl. Beat egg first with a spoon and mix
in other liquid ingredients. Then add dry ingredients and mix until you've
removed all the lumps.

Pour the batter into the mug (do not fill more than halfway) and smooth the
top with a spoon. Thump mug firmly on the tabletop six times to remove
excess air bubbles. Place mug on top of a microwavable small plate or saucer.

Bake for 3 - 4 minutes. Check for doneness by inserting a toothpick in the
middle of the microwave mug cake and removing the toothpick. If the
toothpick is dry, the MMC is done.

Wait 2 minutes, then run a butter knife along the inside of the mug, and tip
the cake into plate. Position the mug cake so that the slightly rounded top
is on top. Your microwave mug cake will now look like a slightly overgrown
muffin.

FANCY STUFF

Frost the whole Tapioca Microwave Mug Cake with whipped cream, or split
the MMC in half, and frost each half individually (in which case you'll end
up with two separate MMCs — or you can reassemble the frosted halves
to create a layered MMC). Decorate, if you wish, with small candies such as
gumdrops or jellybeans.

Triple Chocolate Microwave Mug Cake

INGREDIENTS

1 egg
1 tablespoon chocolate pudding
  (prepared)
2 tablespoons oil
1/8 teaspoon vanilla extract
1/8 teaspoon baking powder
1/4 teaspoon cinnamon
4 tablespoons light brown sugar
2 tablespoons instant chocolate
  pudding powder (not prepared)
4 tablespoons all-purpose flour
2 tablespoons semi-sweet
  chocolate chips

NOTE
The Triple Chocolate Microwave
Mug Cake is referred to by many
as the CCC MMC.

DIRECTIONS

Prepare mug by coating the inside lightly with cooking spray.

Mix the ingredients in a small bowl. Beat egg first with a spoon and mix in other liquid ingredients. Then add dry ingredients and mix until you've removed all the lumps.

Pour the batter into the mug (do not fill more than halfway) and smooth the top with a spoon. Thump mug firmly on the tabletop six times to remove excess air bubbles. Place mug on top of a microwavable small plate or saucer.

Bake for 3 - 4 minutes. Check for doneness by inserting a toothpick in the middle of the microwave mug cake and removing the toothpick. If the toothpick is dry, the MMC is done.

Wait 2 minutes, then run a butter knife along the inside of the mug, and tip the cake into plate. Position the mug cake so that the slightly rounded top is on top. Your microwave mug cake will now look like a slightly overgrown muffin.

FANCY STUFF

Frost the whole Triple Chocolate Microwave Mug Cake with chocolate frosting, or split the MMC in half, and frost each half individually (in which case you'll end up with two separate MMCs — or you can reassemble the frosted halves to create a layered MMC). Decorate, if you wish, with semi-sweet chocolate chips.

Triple Good Microwave Mug Cake

INGREDIENTS

1 egg
1 tablespoon vanilla pudding
(prepared)
2 tablespoons oil
1/8 teaspoon vanilla extract
1/8 teaspoon baking powder
1/4 teaspoon cinnamon
4 tablespoons light brown sugar
2 tablespoons strawberry-flavored
NESQUIK®
4 tablespoons all-purpose flour
2 tablespoons semi-sweet
chocolate chips

NOTE

A scoop of chocolate, vanilla, and strawberry ice cream would compliment the Triple Good Microwave Mug Cake perfectly. Get ours ready now. We'll be over shortly. Thank you in advance.

DIRECTIONS

Prepare mug by coating the inside lightly with cooking spray.

Mix the ingredients in a small bowl. Beat egg first with a spoon and mix in other liquid ingredients. Then add dry ingredients and mix until you've removed all the lumps.

Pour the batter into the mug (do not fill more than halfway) and smooth the top with a spoon. Thump mug firmly on the tabletop six times to remove excess air bubbles. Place mug on top of a microwavable small plate or saucer.

Bake for 3 - 4 minutes. Check for doneness by inserting a toothpick in the middle of the microwave mug cake and removing the toothpick. If the toothpick is dry, the MMC is done.

Wait 2 minutes, then run a butter knife along the inside of the mug, and tip the cake into plate. Position the mug cake so that the slightly rounded top is on top. Your microwave mug cake will now look like a slightly overgrown muffin.

FANCY STUFF

Frost the whole Triple Good Microwave Mug Cake with prepared vanilla pudding or vanilla frosting, or split the MMC in half, and frost each half individually (in which case you'll end up with two separate MMCs — or you can reassemble the frosted halves to create a layered MMC). Decorate, if you wish, with semi-sweet chocolate chips.

Tropical Microwave Mug Cake

INGREDIENTS
1 egg
1 tablespoon pineapple yogurt
(with the fruit stirred in)
1 tablespoon banana yogurt
(with the fruit stirred in)
1 tablespoon oil
1/8 teaspoon coconut extract
1/8 teaspoon baking powder
1/4 teaspoon cinnamon
3 tablespoons light brown sugar
2 tablespoons instant banana
pudding powder (not prepared)
4 tablespoons all-purpose flour
2 tablespoons shredded coconut

NOTE
Our talented cover designer, Kristine, lives on a Caribbean island paradise and probably bakes a Tropical Microwave Mug Cake every day of her life. Except on those days when iguanas crawl into her mug.

DIRECTIONS
Prepare mug by coating the inside lightly with cooking spray.

Mix the ingredients in a small bowl. Beat egg first with a spoon and mix in other liquid ingredients. Then add dry ingredients and mix until you've removed all the lumps.

Pour the batter into the mug (do not fill more than halfway) and smooth the top with a spoon. Thump mug firmly on the tabletop six times to remove excess air bubbles. Place mug on top of a microwavable small plate or saucer.

Bake for 3 - 4 minutes. Check for doneness by inserting a toothpick in the middle of the microwave mug cake and removing the toothpick. If the toothpick is dry, the MMC is done.

Wait 2 minutes, then run a butter knife along the inside of the mug, and tip the cake into plate. Position the mug cake so that the slightly rounded top is on top. Your microwave mug cake will now look like a slightly overgrown muffin.

FANCY STUFF
Frost the whole Tropical Microwave Mug Cake with pineapple yogurt or banana yogurt, or split the MMC in half, and frost each half individually (in which case you'll end up with two separate MMCs — or you can reassemble the frosted halves to create a layered MMC). Decorate, if you wish, with shredded coconut.

Vanilla Peanutbean Microwave Mug Cake

INGREDIENTS
1 egg
1 tablespoon peanut butter
2 tablespoons milk
2 tablespoons oil
1/8 teaspoon vanilla extract
1/8 teaspoon baking powder
1/4 teaspoon cinnamon
4 tablespoons light brown sugar
2 tablespoons instant vanilla
   pudding powder (not prepared)
4 tablespoons all-purpose flour
2 tablespoons jellybeans
   (about 16, carefully cut in half)

NOTE
Use a cutting board when you carefully cut your 16 jellybeans in half, or your mother will yell at you. And if yours doesn't, ours will. Trust me. She will.

DIRECTIONS
Prepare mug by coating the inside lightly with cooking spray.

Mix the ingredients in a small bowl. Beat egg first with a spoon and mix in other liquid ingredients. Then add dry ingredients and mix until you've removed all the lumps.

Pour the batter into the mug (do not fill more than halfway) and smooth the top with a spoon. Thump mug firmly on the tabletop six times to remove excess air bubbles. Place mug on top of a microwavable small plate or saucer.

Bake for 3 - 4 minutes. Check for doneness by inserting a toothpick in the middle of the microwave mug cake and removing the toothpick. If the toothpick is dry, the MMC is done.

Wait 2 minutes, then run a butter knife along the inside of the mug, and tip the cake into plate. Position the mug cake so that the slightly rounded top is on top. Your microwave mug cake will now look like a slightly overgrown muffin.

FANCY STUFF
Frost the whole Vanilla Peanutbean Microwave Mug Cake with peanut butter or with vanilla frosting, or split the MMC in half, and frost each half individually (in which case you'll end up with two separate MMCs — or you can reassemble the frosted halves to create a layered MMC). Decorate, if you wish, with small candies such as gumdrops or jellybeans.

Vanilla Strawberry Microwave Mug Cake

INGREDIENTS

1 egg
2 tablespoons strawberry
   yogurt (with the fruit stirred in)
1 tablespoon oil
1/8 teaspoon vanilla extract
1/8 teaspoon baking powder
1/4 teaspoon cinnamon
4 tablespoons light brown sugar
2 tablespoons instant vanilla
   pudding powder (not prepared)
4 tablespoons all-purpose flour

NOTE
Next Valentine's Day, ask your significant other to bake you a Vanilla Strawberry Microwave Mug Cake. Don't offer to make one. Just ask for one. Let us know what happens.

DIRECTIONS

Prepare mug by coating the inside lightly with cooking spray.

Mix the ingredients in a small bowl. Beat egg first with a spoon and mix in other liquid ingredients. Then add dry ingredients and mix until you've removed all the lumps.

Pour the batter into the mug (do not fill more than halfway) and smooth the top with a spoon. Thump mug firmly on the tabletop six times to remove excess air bubbles. Place mug on top of a microwavable small plate or saucer.

Bake for 3 - 4 minutes. Check for doneness by inserting a toothpick in the middle of the microwave mug cake and removing the toothpick. If the toothpick is dry, the MMC is done.

Wait 2 minutes, then run a butter knife along the inside of the mug, and tip the cake into plate. Position the mug cake so that the slightly rounded top is on top. Your microwave mug cake will now look like a slightly overgrown muffin.

FANCY STUFF

Frost the whole Vanilla Strawberry Microwave Mug Cake with strawberry yogurt or strawberry jelly, or split the MMC in half, and frost each half individually (in which case you'll end up with two separate MMCs — or you can reassemble the frosted halves to create a layered MMC). Decorate, if you wish, with fresh or frozen strawberries.

Velvet Butter Microwave Mug Cake

INGREDIENTS
1 egg
**1 tablespoon peanut butter
(smooth or chunky)**
**1 tablespoon processed cheese
spread (the type you squirt
from a can)**
3 tablespoons oil
1/8 teaspoon vanilla extract
1/8 teaspoon baking powder
4 tablespoons light brown sugar
**2 tablespoons instant vanilla
pudding powder (not prepared)**
4 tablespoons all-purpose flour

NOTE
*Our intrepid MMC testers weren't
too sure about the Velvet Butter
Microwave Mug Cake until we
reminded them of those neon
orange cracker peanut butter
sandwiches they'd grown up with.
Then they came on board.*

DIRECTIONS
Prepare mug by coating the inside lightly with cooking spray.

Mix the ingredients in a small bowl. Beat egg first with a spoon and mix
in other liquid ingredients. Then add dry ingredients and mix until you've
removed all the lumps.

Pour the batter into the mug (do not fill more than halfway) and smooth the
top with a spoon. Thump mug firmly on the tabletop six times to remove
excess air bubbles. Place mug on top of a microwavable small plate or saucer.

Bake for 3 - 4 minutes. Check for doneness by inserting a toothpick in the
middle of the microwave mug cake and removing the toothpick. If the
toothpick is dry, the MMC is done.

Wait 2 minutes, then run a butter knife along the inside of the mug, and tip
the cake into plate. Position the mug cake so that the slightly rounded top
is on top. Your microwave mug cake will now look like a slightly overgrown
muffin.

FANCY STUFF
Frost the whole Velvet Butter Microwave Mug Cake with peanut butter, or
split the MMC in half, and frost each half individually (in which case you'll end
up with two separate MMCs — or you can reassemble the frosted halves to
create a layered MMC). Decorate, if you wish, with dabs of processed cheese
spread.

Watermelon Ginger Microwave Mug Cake

INGREDIENTS

1 egg
3 tablespoons milk
3 tablespoons oil
1/8 teaspoon vanilla extract
1/8 teaspoon baking powder
1/4 teaspoon ginger
4 tablespoons light brown sugar
2 tablespoons watermelon instant
  gelatin powder (not prepared)
4 tablespoons all-purpose flour

NOTE
The best thing about watermelon gelatin is that there are no seeds to spit out. So, if you're eating a Watermelon Ginger Microwave Mug Cake, and you're spitting out seeds, then you screwed up the recipe. Either that, or something disgusting fell into your mug.

DIRECTIONS

Prepare mug by coating the inside lightly with cooking spray.

Mix the ingredients in a small bowl. Beat egg first with a spoon and mix in other liquid ingredients. Then add dry ingredients and mix until you've removed all the lumps.

Pour the batter into the mug (do not fill more than halfway) and smooth the top with a spoon. Thump mug firmly on the tabletop six times to remove excess air bubbles. Place mug on top of a microwavable small plate or saucer.

Bake for 3 - 4 minutes. Check for doneness by inserting a toothpick in the middle of the microwave mug cake and removing the toothpick. If the toothpick is dry, the MMC is done.

Wait 2 minutes, then run a butter knife along the inside of the mug, and tip the cake into plate. Position the mug cake so that the slightly rounded top is on top. Your microwave mug cake will now look like a slightly overgrown muffin.

FANCY STUFF

Frost the whole Watermelon Ginger Microwave Mug Cake with whipped cream, or split the MMC in half, and frost each half individually (in which case you'll end up with two separate MMCs — or you can reassemble the frosted halves to create a layered MMC). Decorate, if you wish, with small candies such as gumdrops or jellybeans.

White Grapeberry Microwave Mug Cake

INGREDIENTS

1 egg

2 tablespoons mixed strawberry yogurt (with the fruit stirred in)

1 tablespoon oil

1/8 teaspoon vanilla extract

1/8 teaspoon baking powder

1/4 teaspoon cinnamon

4 tablespoons light brown sugar

1 tablespoon White Grape Crystal Light powder (that's one individual package)

5 tablespoons all-purpose flour

NOTE

Once you've finished baking and cooling your White Grapeberry Microwave Mug Cake, you can always transfer it to a crystal plate — assuming you've always envied those felines from that cat food commercial.

DIRECTIONS

Prepare mug by coating the inside lightly with cooking spray.

Mix the ingredients in a small bowl. Beat egg first with a spoon and mix in other liquid ingredients. Then add dry ingredients and mix until you've removed all the lumps.

Pour the batter into the mug (do not fill more than halfway) and smooth the top with a spoon. Thump mug firmly on the tabletop six times to remove excess air bubbles. Place mug on top of a microwavable small plate or saucer.

Bake for 3 - 4 minutes. Check for doneness by inserting a toothpick in the middle of the microwave mug cake and removing the toothpick. If the toothpick is dry, the MMC is done.

Wait 2 minutes, then run a butter knife along the inside of the mug, and tip the cake into plate. Position the mug cake so that the slightly rounded top is on top. Your microwave mug cake will now look like a slightly overgrown muffin.

FANCY STUFF

Frost the whole White Grapeberry Microwave Mug Cake with strawberry jelly, or the rest of the strawberry yogurt, or split the MMC in half, and frost each half individually (in which case you'll end up with two separate MMCs — or you can reassemble the frosted halves to create a layered MMC). Decorate, if you wish, with fresh or frozen strawberries.

Yogurt Raisin Microwave Mug Cake

INGREDIENTS

1 egg
2 tablespoons Greek yogurt
  (plain)
1 tablespoon oil
1/8 teaspoon vanilla extract
1/8 teaspoon baking powder
1/4 teaspoon cinnamon
4 tablespoons light brown sugar
2 tablespoons instant vanilla
  pudding powder (not prepared)
4 tablespoons all-purpose flour
2 tablespoons raisins

NOTE
Does a container of yogurt have to join a fraternity or a sorority if it wants to wear a Greek letter?

DIRECTIONS

Prepare mug by coating the inside lightly with cooking spray.

Mix the ingredients in a small bowl. Beat egg first with a spoon and mix in other liquid ingredients. Then add dry ingredients and mix until you've removed all the lumps.

Pour the batter into the mug (do not fill more than halfway) and smooth the top with a spoon. Thump mug firmly on the tabletop six times to remove excess air bubbles. Place mug on top of a microwavable small plate or saucer.

Bake for 3 - 4 minutes. Check for doneness by inserting a toothpick in the middle of the microwave mug cake and removing the toothpick. If the toothpick is dry, the MMC is done.

Wait 2 minutes, then run a butter knife along the inside of the mug, and tip the cake into plate. Position the mug cake so that the slightly rounded top is on top. Your microwave mug cake will now look like a slightly overgrown muffin.

FANCY STUFF

Frost the whole Yogurt Raisin Microwave Mug Cake with whipped cream or vanilla frosting, or split the MMC in half, and frost each half individually (in which case you'll end up with two separate MMCs — or you can reassemble the frosted halves to create a layered MMC). Decorate, if you wish, with raisins.

We'd love your feedback.
Please visit www.microwavemugcakes.com and become part of the Microwave Mug Cakes community!